Journey to Greatness

Lessons from the Life of Joseph

Lynne Modranski

I0088563

More by Lynne Modranski

Jesus, Teach Me How to Pray

Heroes, Heroines Champs and Chumps

Children of the King

Fruit of the Spirit

Journey to Greatness
Lessons from the Life of Joseph

©2021 Lynne Modranski
www.LynneModranski.com

All rights reserved. No part of this publication may be reproduced, distributed, or transmitted in any form or by any means, including photocopying, recording, or other electronic or mechanical methods, without the prior written permission of the publisher, except in the case of brief quotations embodied in critical reviews and certain other noncommercial uses permitted by copyright law.

EXCEPTION: The original purchasing local church or individual home school family may reproduce any and every part of this curriculum for use in their ministry/teaching setting, including copies for churches who use multiple teachers/ministry leaders. Please do not share with other churches or families.

Published by Mansion Hill Press
Steubenville, Ohio
www.MansionHillPress.com

ISBN: 978-1-953374-06-6

Scripture in this curriculum has been copied or paraphrased from:
THE HOLY BIBLE, NEW INTERNATIONAL VERSION®, NIV® Copyright © 1973, 1978, 1984, 2011 by Biblica, Inc.® Used by permission. All rights reserved worldwide.

The Holman Christian Standard Bible®, Copyright © 1999, 2000, 2002, 2003, 2009 by Holman Bible Publishers. Used by permission. Holman Christian Standard Bible®, Holman CSB®, and HCSB® are federally registered trademarks of Holman Bible Publishers.

The New Century Version®. Copyright © 2005 by Thomas Nelson. Used by permission. All rights reserved.

The Sycamore Tree Series

This curriculum is one of many originally written for and used by
Sycamore Tree Ministries in Follansbee, WV.

Look for the Sycamore Tree Series banner on other
Children's Curriculum and Bible Discussion Guides

Special thanks to the ministry leaders and
children for testing and learning from these studies.

You're always my first audience!

OVERVIEW

The life of Joseph offers many lessons for children as well as adults.
During the next eleven sessions, kids in your ministry will explore these themes:

SUPPLIES NEEDED

General Supplies

Crayons
Markers
Scissors
Construction Paper
Glue/Glue Sticks

Masking/Painters Tape
Transparent Tape
Pens/Pencils
String/Yarn
Pipe Cleaners

White Board & Markers

Nearly every lesson will
need some copies

Special Supplies

Lesson One
Stuffed Animals
Craft Visors
Craft Gems
Puffy Paint

Lesson Two
Pillow
Tongue Depressors

Lesson Three
Plastic Lacing Cord
Black & White Pony Beads
Heart Pony Beads

Lesson Four
Cereal or Tissue boxes
Felt

Safety or Butterfly Pins
Small Foam Crosses
Small colored discs/chips
Sharpie
Basket

Lesson Five
Wooden Blocks
Nerf Balls or balled paper
Elastic Cord
Pony Beads
Letter Beads

Lesson Six
Hard Boiled Eggs
Spoons
Broken Egg Shells

Lesson Seven
Sticky Gems

Lesson Eight
Tubular Pasta
Recorded Music

Lesson Ten
Photos of kids in poverty
Rice, Oats, dried grains
2 large Bowls
Plastic Spoons

Lesson Eleven
Index Cards
Poster/Tag Board
Empty Soda Bottles
Craft Paint

Each lesson offers the following components to help you prepare and offer a full ministry time with your group. If you have less than an hour, use the Bible Lesson, and then pick two or three activities depending on your time frame.

Notes, Scribbles, Jots & Doodles

⇒ **INTRODUCTION/LEADER'S DEVOTION**

This short narrative gives the adult leader a general overview of the scripture and the theme for the session

⇒ **OPENING ACTIVITY**

An object lesson or discussion to set up the Bible story

⇒ **BIBLE LESSON**

You'll explore some part of Joseph's life during every session. I encourage leaders to have their Bible open to the correct scripture then paraphrase it in their own words to make it easier for children to understand. Each lesson has a paraphrase that can be read by leaders who aren't comfortable telling the story on their own. Be sure to ask questions throughout the lesson and allow for answers. This will help keep the children's attention.

⇒ **HELPING THEM REMEMBER**

Each session offers at least four ways to reinforce the theme. Choose the ones that will work best for your group. If you rotate teachers, I recommend each teacher use the ones that best fit their personality. This will allow a nice mix of activities for the kids.

⇒ **CRAFT**
⇒ **MEMORY VERSE**
⇒ **GAME**
⇒ **ACTIVITY**

These range from songs, coloring sheets, videos, stories and more

⇒ **CLOSING MOMENTS**

Kids need to learn to be responsible. So each time we'll encourage them to clean up their mess. Then we'll close in prayer. A suggested prayer is offered, but teachers could prayer spontaneously

A Note to Ministry Leaders

Thank you for leading in this important ministry. With all the worldly things influencing children today, they need Godly instruction more than ever before. As these young people begin to see we love them with the love of Jesus Christ, they'll be more likely to accept Him as their Savior. We help them develop a healthy self-worth; and as they grow into teens, we become layers of accountability. When a child has a group of adults to potentially disappoint, they'll be less likely to follow the crowd.

As you prepare, try to read the scripture and the short overview early in the week even if you don't have time to get the entire lesson ready. Allow Joseph's story to change you before it changes the children. If you rotate lessons, take some time to familiarize yourself with the chapters of Genesis proceeding the verses you'll use. Joseph's story begins in Genesis 37.

I also recommend looking over the supply list early in the week so you can gather any extra materials or let your ministry coordinator know what you need.

You'll see that each lesson includes a summarized story to share with the children. You may use this or share the Bible lesson in your own words making sure you emphasize the theme for the week. Each activity will reinforce the lesson so sharing the small section following the activity is important.

Above all be in prayer for the children in your ministry. Ask the Holy Spirit to lead you as you prepare and teach. Pray for each of them by name asking God to call them to Him and to help them develop a personal relationship with Jesus Christ. On the next page, I'll share a short, child sized version of the Roman's Road to Salvation in case you need help leading a child to Christ.

Thanks again for being a role model for these children. May Christ bless you richly as you help them find their way to Him.

The Roman's Road to Salvation for Children

Romans 3:10 & 23

"There is no one righteous, not even one." "For all have sinned and fallen short of the glory of God."

This can be a difficult concept for your more well-behaved kids to understand. In fact, it's tough for most respectable adults. But that's because we compare ourselves to other humans instead of our Creator. Basically for a child, if we just explain, no one is perfect like Jesus, and we need to admit we're not perfect, they'll get it.

Romans 5:8

"God demonstrated His love for us in this: While we were yet sinners, Christ died for us."

Even though we aren't perfect, God loves us anyway. Every sin needs a sacrifice to make us right with God. So Jesus came to be our sacrifice.

Romans 6:23

"For the wages of sin is death, but the gift of God is eternal life."

We get to choose. Some people think God condemns people to hell, but the Almighty gives us a choice. We can choose to try to work for our salvation and reap the wages of eternal dying, or we can choose to follow Jesus Christ, and open the gift of eternal life. Help kids understand God wants to give us life with Him forever. He sent Jesus to pay our way there. When we love Jesus, we naturally begin to do the right thing.

Romans 10:9-10

"If you confess with your mouth, "Jesus is Lord" and believe in your heart that God raised Him from the dead, you will be saved [from sin and death]. For it is with your heart that you believe and are justified and it is with your mouth that you confess and are saved."

Ask the child, "Do you believe Jesus died to pay for your sin?" If they say yes, they have confessed with their mouth. Ask them if they'd like to ask Jesus to change their heart and make them more like Him. The lead them in prayer. I'll give a suggested prayer below, but it doesn't have to be this exact prayer. After you pray with the child, help him or her decide who they will tell about their salvation. We can't keep it to ourselves, but it's important to help kids start giving their testimony to safe people so they won't be discouraged by scoffers and non-believers.

Here's that prayer I promised:

Dear Jesus, I am a sinner in need of a Savior. I know that you love me, and you died on the cross for me so my sins can be forgiven. Please forgive me for (now share some of your sins with Jesus to show your sincerity). Thank you for giving your life for mine. Thank you for raising from the dead so I could have a new life. Please be with me always. I want you to control my life, change my heart, and help me live my life for you. In Jesus name, AMEN

The Life of Joseph

Lesson One: The Favorite Son

INTRODUCTION/LEADER'S DEVOTION

Being the favorite can be fun. Preferential treatment and special gifts make it exciting, and sometimes we even get away with more mistakes. Unfortunately, being the favorite can also be difficult. It can come with name calling and contempt. The favorite often becomes arrogant as he lets his status go to his head. I wonder if that's what happened to Joseph?

At age seventeen, he'd been his dad's favorite since the day he was born. Jacob had waited a long time for his beloved Rachel to get pregnant. The first son of his preferred wife, Joseph held a special place in his father's heart. I'm guessing the robe was just one of many ways Jacob showed favoritism to his eleventh son, and I'm wondering if tattling on his older brothers was one way Joseph's arrogance rubbed his brothers the wrong way.

The Bible says God doesn't show favoritism. Unlike humans God can have many favorites without showing partiality toward any of us.

Like Joseph we are the favorite. Our Heavenly Father loves us like we were his only child. But like Joseph, it's easy to become arrogant about our status. It's helpful to remember God has more than one favorite. Today as we help the children understand they are God's favorite, be reminded you are His favorite too!

OVERVIEW

OPENING ACTIVITY   5 Minutes

Choosing A Favorite

Materials Needed: A box filled with a variety of stuffed animals and toys, enough for each child to choose one and a few extras

BIBLE LESSON   10 Minutes

Genesis 37:1-4

HELPING THEM REMEMBER

MEMORY VERSE   15 Minutes

Psalm 139:14 - Heart Chain

Materials Needed: Construction Paper (some precut in 1" x 6" strips, write the memory verse on strips for the younger children, precut some into 1" - 1.5" hearts), scissors, markers

GAME   5-10 Minutes

God's Favorite

Materials Needed: Heart pillow or other small stuffed heart or animal, Music (a song like "Who You Say I Am" by Hillsong United)

CRAFT   10-20 Minutes

Richly Ornamented Visor

Materials Needed: Craft Visors, Stick-on Gems, Puffy Paint, Markers, etc.

ACTIVITY   5-10 Minutes

Coloring Sheet: Joseph's Fancy Robe

Materials Needed: Copies of the Coloring Sheet from the last page and crayons

CLOSING MOMENTS   5 Minutes

Clean Up and Prayer Time

The Life of Joseph - Lesson One: The Favorite Son

OPENING ACTIVITY   5 Minutes

Choosing A Favorite

Materials Needed: A box filled with a variety of stuffed animals and toys, enough for each child to choose one and a few extras

Preparation: Set all of the toys on a table. As the children arrive, have them pick their favorite.

WHAT TO DO: After every child has chosen a toy, ask these questions allowing for short discussion:

1. Did everyone get their favorite or had someone else already taken your favorite?

2. Which of the favorites is the best favorite? *(This should cause a stir. Everyone should think their favorite is the best.)*

3. Can we have more than one favorite in our class? *(There will be mixed reactions. Some children will want more than one favorite, others will be convinced, favorite implies only one.)*

4. How does it feel to know everyone doesn't want the toy you picked to be the class favorite?

SAY: Today we're going to learn about a boy who was his dad's favorite. I'm going to tell you about Joseph. *(If children can hold their toy without much fidgeting, you might let them hang on to it during the lesson. This could be a good opportunity to help children learn to sit quietly. If the toy becomes distracting during the story, ask them once to stop, and if they continue, have them put the toy in the box. Remind them we sit quietly so everyone can learn together. Becoming a distraction is not polite. If your group has a difficult time sitting still during the story, have them put the toys in the box and let them color the activity sheet while you share Joseph's story.)*

BIBLE LESSON   10 Minutes

Genesis 37:1-4 - Joseph Gets His Robe

Read Genesis 37:1-4 as you prepare. Have your Bible open as you tell the story to remind the children this Joseph is a real person from Scripture. Retell the story in your own words or use the dialogue below

Jacob lived a long time ago. He had 12 sons, one of them was named Joseph. This isn't Jesus' dad, this Joseph lived about 2000 years before Jesus.

Jacob was very old by the time Joseph was born, and even though he was Jacob's eleventh son, Joseph was his father's favorite. To show how much he loved Joseph, Jacob bought him a very fancy robe. It wasn't an ordinary robe. It probably made Joseph feel very special.

One day when Joseph was about seventeen, he was helping some of his older brothers take care of the sheep. When he got home he told his dad his brothers weren't doing it the right way. How do you think that made his brothers feel? *(allow for answers)* How does it make you feel when someone else is the favorite and they tattle on you? *(allow for answers)*

Did you know you are as special to God as Joseph was to Jacob? You are God's favorite. But God is different than you and me because God can have many favorites. Would you like to be God's favorite? *(allow for answers, then move to the memory verse)*

10

HELPING THEM REMEMBER

MEMORY VERSE   15 Minutes

Psalm 139:14 - Heart Chain

Materials Needed: Construction Paper (for each child precut seven 1" x 6" strips and 2-4 1"-1.5" hearts - write the memory verse on five strips for the younger children - leave some blank for older kids), scissors, markers

I praise you ♦ because you made me ♦ in an amazing ♦ and wonderful way.

Psalm 139:14

SAY: You are God's favorite because He made you. The Bible says, "I praise You because You made me in an amazing and wonderful way!" Let's say that together. *(Break the verse into four parts. Use the diamonds as a guide. Recite the first part, asking the children to repeat it, then the second, third and fourth. Do this two or three times, then break the verse in two parts and have them repeat it after you. Ask if any can recite the entire verse by themselves when you are done.)*

DO: Give each child seven strips of construction paper. If you have a longer class time, you can let older children cut their own strips and hearts. Let older children write the memory verse on five strips *(include the reference)*. Have each child glue one or two hearts onto the blank strips. Then join the strips into a paper chain, placing a blank strip on each end. Decorate your learning space with your chain.

SAY: We're going to leave this chain hang for several weeks as a reminder God made us each very special, and we are God's favorite.

GAME   5-10 Minutes

God's Favorite

Materials Needed: Heart pillow or other small stuffed heart or animal, Music (a song like "Who You Say I Am" by Hillsong United)

DO: Have kids sit in a circle on the floor, then explain:

SAY: I'm going to give this stuffed heart to one person in the circle. When the music starts, he'll pass it to the next person and say, "I am God's Favorite, yes, I am!" the next person will say, "You ARE God's favorite, yes, you are!" Every time you are passing the heart off, you'll say, "I am God's favorite," and every time you take the heart you'll say, "You ARE God's favorite." I'm going to play music softly while you pass the heart, when the music stops, the one holding the heart will sit in the center of the circle.

DO: Start the music and give the stuffed heart to the first child. Help the first few kids with the lines. After they have the hang of it, stop the music and move one of the children to sit in the center of the circle. As children move to the center, have them sit with their backs to one another. Continue until only one child remains on the outside. Then have that child hand off to a person inside the circle and keep the game going with the children inside the circle. Have the child holding the heart when the music stops move to the outside of the circle again. The game ends when there is only one person left inside the circle.

SAY: How did it feel to be put in the center of the circle? *(allow for answers - most children will feel bad they got out)*

Were you surprised when the game continued after everyone was on the inside of the circle? How did you feel then? *(allow for answers)*

Were you ever really out of the game? *(No)*

Just like when you thought you were out of the game, but you weren't, sometimes it doesn't feel like you're God's favorite, but you are! Even when you feel bad or you've done something wrong, you are still God's favorite!

CRAFT   10-20 Minutes

Richly Ornamented Visor
Materials Needed: Craft Visors, Stick-on Gems, Puffy Paint, Markers, etc.

SAY: What did Joseph have that his brothers didn't? *(Allow for answers - A fancy robe)* Today you're going to make your own fancy clothing. We're going to decorate these visors so we have something fancy to wear!

DO: Give each child a visor and decorating supplies

Help kids decorate their visors

SAY: How do you think wearing his robe made Joseph feel? *(No wrong answers)* I think he felt very special. It feels good to know someone loves us. That's why we made this visor, so you will remember how much God loves you. I want you to always remember you are God's favorite.

ACTIVITY   5-10 Minutes

Coloring Sheet: Joseph's Fancy Robe
Materials Needed: Copies of the Coloring Sheet from the next page and crayons

If you have children who can't read in your group, prepare your pages by using crayons to color code the words on the coloring sheet. This could alternately be a take home sheet. If you have a group whose attention is difficult to keep during the story, you could allow them to color this page during that time. If not, use the dialogue below as they color.

SAY: We don't know what Joseph's coat looked like, but the Bible does tell us it was fancier than most robes. Some people call it Joseph's Coat of Many Colors. *(You can ask the questions below, repeating the correct answer when a child gives it)*

- Who can tell me how Joseph got his coat? *His Father gave it to him*

- Why did Joseph's dad give him the beautiful robe? *Joseph was his favorite*

- How do you think that made his brothers feel? *No wrong answers*

- Who calls you his favorite? *This may be a parent or aunt, but eventually remind them they are God's favorite*

CLOSING MOMENTS   5 Minutes

Clean Up and Prayer Time

Encourage the children to clean up their ministry space and then close with the prayer in the column to the right or pray spontaneously.

Dear God,

I praise you that I am your favorite, and that each of these kids is your favorite too! Forgive us when we forget and help us to show others that they are your favorite too.

In Jesus' Name we pray, Amen

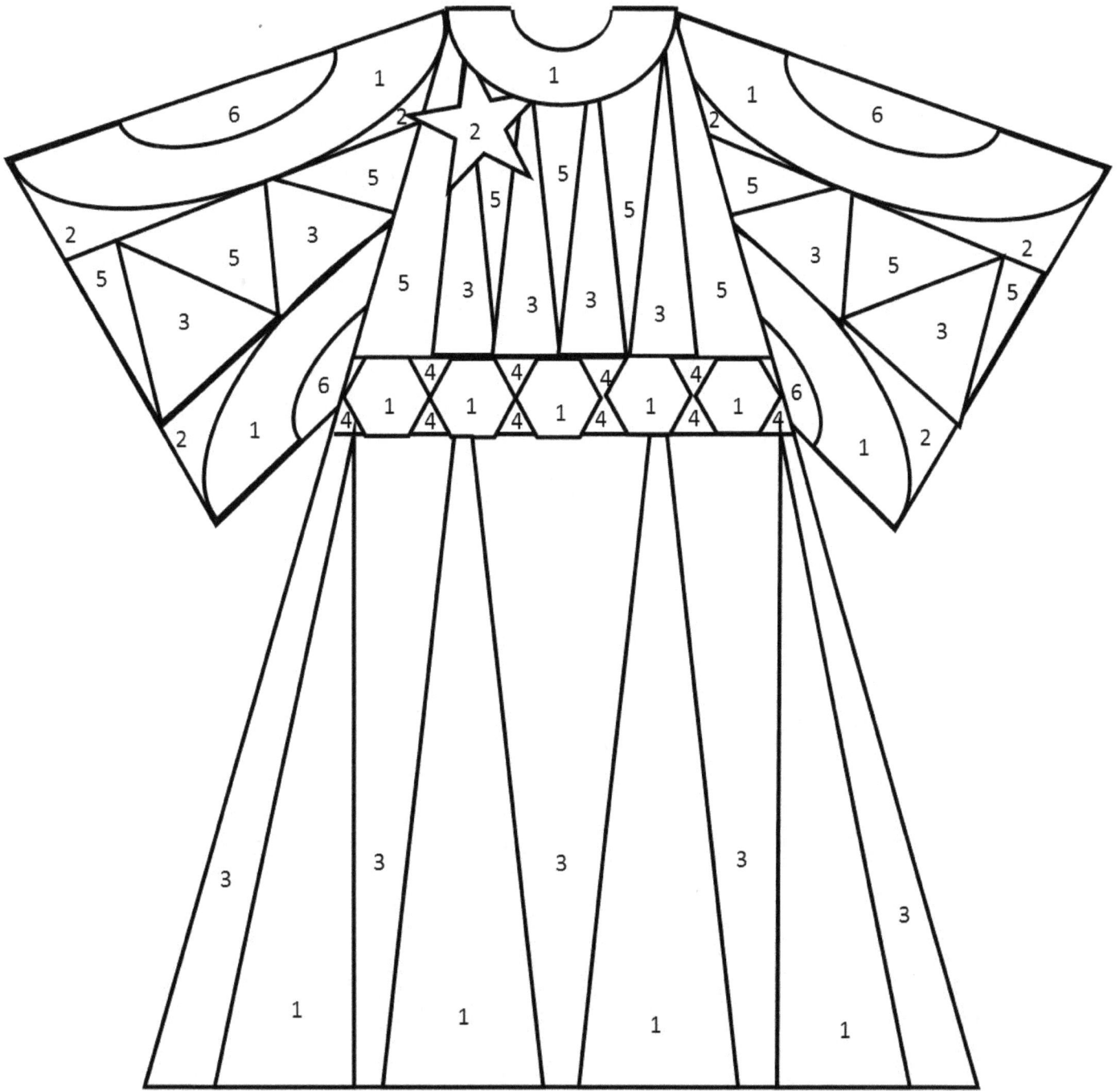

Color Joseph's Ornamented Coat

We don't know what it really looked like, but this is pretty fancy!

1 - Red   4 - Orange

2 - Yellow   5 - Green

3 - Blue   6 - Purple

Intentionally left blank
so if you print from PDF
or tear the lesson out of the book
the next lesson falls on a fresh page

The Life of Joseph

Lesson Two: Staying Humble Even When You're the Favorite

INTRODUCTION/LEADER'S DEVOTION

Joseph was a dreamer. Perhaps his father's lavish attention made him too big for his britches. We know he was a tattle-tale and not so popular with his brothers, so you'd think when God gave him these two dreams, wisdom may have told him to share the visions discreetly. Yet, Joseph told everyone about his seemingly arrogant dreams.

God gave Joseph two dreams, in one he and his brothers were stalks of wheat, and in the another they were stars. Both dreams featured Joseph's stalk and star being bowed to. When he told his family the outlandish stories, his half-brothers became even more estranged.

This week Joseph can teach us what not to do. After discovering God favors us, it's important to remember God can have more than one favorite. Humility will take us far and help win others to Christ. Arrogance drives people away. Even though you are definitely God's favorite, Joseph's story reminds us not to lord it over others and stay humble.

OVERVIEW

OPENING ACTIVITY   5 Minutes
    Let's Talk About Your Dreams
    Materials Needed: Pillow

BIBLE LESSON   10 Minutes
    Genesis 37:5-11

HELPING THEM REMEMBER

    MEMORY VERSE   5 Minutes
        James 4:10

    GAME   5-10 Minutes
        Humility Scavenger Hunt
        Materials Needed: Copies of the cards at the back of this lesson (one set per student - each student could have a different color if you like) and a small trash can

    CRAFT   10-20 Minutes
        Dream Cloud Mobile
        Materials Needed: Cards from game or Construction Paper, Tongue Depressors, Tape, Yarn.

    ACTIVITY   5-10 Minutes
        Coloring Sheet - Joseph's Dreams
        Materials Needed: Coloring Sheet and Crayons

CLOSING MOMENTS   5 Minutes
    Clean Up and Prayer Time

The Life of Joseph - Lesson Two:
Staying Humble Even When You're the Favorite

OPENING ACTIVITY   5 Minutes

Let's Talk About Your Dreams
Materials Needed: Pillow

WHAT TO DO: Show children your pillow

SAY: What is this? (*allow for answers*) What do you use it for? (*Allow for answers*) Do any of you have dreams when you're using one of these? (*Allow for answers and encourage children to share some of their dreams or even nightmares.*) Did anyone ever get mad at you because of your dreams? (*Allow for answers*) Today we're going to talk about a man from the Bible who had some dreams. But his dreams made his brothers angry.

BIBLE LESSON   10 Minutes

Genesis 37:5-11

Read Genesis 37:5-11 as you prepare.
Have your Bible open as you tell the story
to remind the children this Joseph is a real person from Scripture.
Retell the story in your own words or use the dialogue below

What do you remember about Joseph from last week? (*Allow for answers. Be sure someone says Joseph was his father's favorite, and Jacob gave him a beautiful robe/coat to wear. Remind them they are God's favorites*) Do you remember how many brothers Joseph had? (*11*) And how did Joseph's brothers feel about him? (*His brothers didn't like him much*)

No, Joseph's brothers didn't really like him. They were jealous because he was their dad's favorite. And some people who don't follow Jesus might not like it when they find out God loves us so much, even though God loves them just as much; they just don't realize it!

Joseph had a dream. In this dream he and his eleven brothers were out in the field binding grain. Do you know what it looks like when farmers bind grain by hand and don't have machines? (*Show the picture at the end of this lesson*) Farmers cut the tall grain and then bundle a bunch of it together. The big bundles will stand up by themselves.

Joseph dreamt he and his brothers each had created a bundle of grain. In his dream his brothers' bundles bowed down to his bundle like he was the king or something. How do you think that made his brothers feel? (*Allow for answers*)

The Bible says his brothers hated him even more. But if that wasn't bad enough, Joseph had another dream, and again he shared it with his brothers as well as his dad and step-mom. This time the sun, moon and eleven stars all bowed down to Joseph. His family knew the dream meant Joseph thought they'd all bow down to him one day. The sun represented his dad, the moon stood for his step-mom and the eleven stars were his brothers.

By this time even his dad said, "Enough." His dad laughed at him, "Do you really think your whole family is going to bow down to you?" His brothers were even more jealous, but his dad remembered the dreams for a long time.

Why do you think Joseph told his brothers his dreams? (*Probably just to show off*)

Should Joseph have bragged about what he saw? *(It would have been better for the family relations if he'd kept the dreams to himself)*

Joseph wasn't very humble. When we brag about what we've done or boast about being God's favorite, how does that make others feel? *(It's OK to share accomplishments, but when we brag trying to make ourselves better than others, it makes our friends feel bad)* Do you think God likes it when we brag and boast just to make ourselves feel better? *(No, God wants us to always think of others' feelings)*

HELPING THEM REMEMBER

MEMORY VERSE   5 Minutes

James 4:10

Humble yourselves in the sight of the Lord, and He will lift you up.

James 4:10

DO: Find the song with this verse on YouTube prior to class. Be sure to cue past any ads. This is my favorite version:
https://www.youtube.com/watch?v=sU8MAQKSbEI
Play the video about 1/2 way through (until the entire memory verse has played) and then invite the children to sing along.

SAY: What does James tell us God will do for us when we're humble? *(Allow for answers)* God will lift us up. When we humble ourselves, we think about ourselves less, but God thinks about us even more.

GAME   5-10 Minutes

Humility Scavenger Hunt
Materials Needed: Copies of the cards at the back of this lesson (one set per student - each student could have a different color if you'd like) and a small trash can

DO: Before class begins, cut the cards apart and hide them around your ministry area. Save one set to show the children what they're looking for.

SAY: Today we're going to find words to help us understand humble better. Hidden around the room you'll find cards with words. Six of the cards have words describing a humble person, these cards have hearts on them. *(Show a couple of these cards)* When you find these cards hold on to them. *(If you created a different color for each student let them know to only find one color of card)* Two of the cards do not describe a humble person. *(Show these two cards)* When you find these cards, bring them here and throw them in this little trash can. Make sure you find each word only one time.

After the children have found their cards:

SAY: What are the words on your cards? *(Allow older kids to read the words)* What are the words on the cards we threw away? *(Allow for answers)* Was Joseph kind and gentle, giving and gracious when he shared his dreams? *(Allow for answers - encourage them to say no)* Joseph was young, and since he was his dad's favorite, he forgot to be humble. Even though we're God's favorite, we must remember to be humble.

CRAFT

Dream Cloud Mobile

Materials Needed: Cards from game or Construction Paper, Tongue depressors, Tape, Yarn.

DO: If you have the cards from the game, help children cut these into cloud shapes (or cut them into cloud shapes when you're preparing for the game). Otherwise give students construction paper and help them cut out 6 - 8 clouds (patterns below) and write one humble description on each. Then follow these steps:

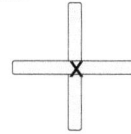

1. Leaving a 6" tail, use yarn to tie together two tongue depressors perpendicular to one another. (the yarn should make an "x" around the sticks) tie a knot close to the sticks, then cut the ends to about 3 inches and tie a knot to make a hanger.

2. Attach a six inch piece of yarn to each cloud with tape.

3. Tie one cloud to each end of each stick. If you made 8 clouds tie a second about half way to the center of each end. If you use 6 clouds, put them across from each other for balance

SAY: You can hang this Dream Cloud Mobile in your room to remind you to be kind and gentle, giving and gracious every day. It should help you remember to always share the credit and be trustworthy. Being God's favorite is exciting, but He wants us to stay humble.

ACTIVITY   5-10 Minutes

Activity Sheet - Joseph's Dreams
Materials Needed: Activity Sheet and Crayons

You can use the activity sheet at the end of this lesson while you tell the Bible story or as a separate activity. When you have a "busier" group sometimes giving them something to do with their hands will help them pay more attention to the lesson.

DO: Pass out the activity sheet. The children will draw the sheaves of wheat bowing to Joseph's sheaf (pictured) and the stars and the sun and the moon bowing to the pictured star. They'll find a couple of bowing stars and sheaves to get them started.

SAY: How many sheaves and stars do we need to draw? *(Allow for answers. Correct answer is 11)* Why that many? *(Allow for answers.)* Why did Joseph dream the sun and the moon would bow to him? *(Allow for answers.)* Do you think anything like this will ever happen? *(Allow for answers, but don't let those who know the story give away the ending yet. Let them know we'll be talking about that in the weeks to come)*

CLOSING MOMENTS   5 Minutes
Clean Up and Prayer Time

Encourage the children to clean up their ministry space and then close with the prayer below or pray spontaneously.

Heavenly Father,
Thank you so much that I am your favorite. I am grateful for your blessings. Help me, Lord, to never allow my status as favorite to go to my head. Remind me to be humble like Jesus so I can always be kind and giving, gentle and gracious. I want to always share the credit and be trustworthy. Thank you for lifting me up when I am humble. In the name of Jesus we pray, Amen.

This is a picture of Wheat Sheaves to show the students so they better understand what Joseph's dream entailed.

Kind

Gentle

Giving

Shares the credit

Gracious

Trust-worthy

Mean

Selfish

Joseph's Dreams

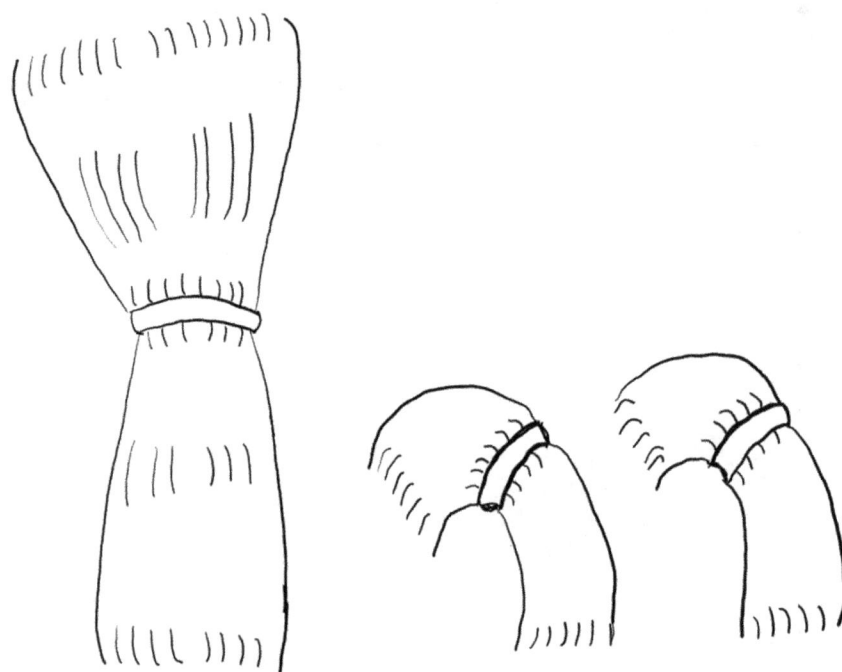

The Life of Joseph

Lesson Three: When People Treat You Badly

INTRODUCTION/LEADER'S DEVOTION

Joseph, the son of the favorite wife, continued to be a thorn in his brothers' sides. In addition to the dreams and the ornate jacket, while they were 80 miles away keeping track of herds of animals, perhaps separated from their own children, Joseph stayed home with dad. Since Jacob's oldest son was at least 30, you'd think he'd have outgrown this childish rivalry, but even if he had, he was powerless to keep the younger siblings, ranging in age from 20-30, reigned in.

So when Joseph showed up to check on them, the brothers weren't very welcoming. In fact, they plotted to kill him. Fortunately, Judah had enough sense to know a bad idea when he heard it. But his solution sent Joseph to Egypt as a slave.

What do we do when people are out to get us? It seems impossible. We can choose to focus on the wrongs committed or focus on what God can do. When we narrow our vision to God's promises, the bullying doesn't go away, but we can see past what the bullying has caused and realize our Heavenly Father has better things in store.

OVERVIEW

OPENING ACTIVITY   5 Minutes
　Have You Been Bullied or Are You the Bully? Discussion

BIBLE LESSON   10 Minutes
　Genesis 37:12-35

HELPING THEM REMEMBER

　MEMORY VERSE   5 Minutes
　　Matthew 5:44

　ACTIVITY   5-10 Minutes
　　Am I a Bully?
　　Materials Needed: Scrap Paper, White Board, Pencils

　GAME   5-10 Minutes
　　Throw Away the Bad Names
　　Materials Needed: Paper from Activity, Masking/Painters Tape

　CRAFT   10-25 Minutes
　　Love Your Enemies Bracelet
　　Materials Needed: Plastic Lacing Cord, Heart Beads, Black Pony Beads, White Pony Beads.

CLOSING MOMENTS   5 Minutes
　Clean Up and Prayer Time

OPENING ACTIVITY   5 Minutes

Have You Been Bullied or Are You the Bully? Discussion

In this discussion, be prepared to hear troubling scenarios, perhaps even about parents or other adults who should be on the trusted list. If you feel a child is endangered by an adult, please talk to the pastor or be prepared to report the incident.

SAY: We've been learning about Joseph. What do you remember about him? *(Affirm any correct answers. Make sure someone says, "He was his dad's favorite" and "His brothers didn't like him because he was his dad's favorite")*

How do you think Joseph felt knowing his brothers didn't like him? *(Allow for answers)*

It would be difficult knowing your brothers or sisters didn't like you. How do you think Joseph's brothers treated him? *(Allow for answers. Help the kids realize they probably didn't treat him well)*

Have you ever been treated badly by someone? *(Allow for answers and encourage the children to share stories. Do not allow them to get graphic.)*

Have you ever treated anyone badly? *(Encourage discussion. If a child is brave enough to share, thank them, then ask them if it was the right things to do. Then ask if they apologized. If they didn't, encourage them to do so. Do not allow this to become a right to brag.)*

Today we're going to talk about a time when Joseph's brothers treated him very badly.

BIBLE LESSON   10 Minutes

Genesis 37:12-35

Read Genesis 37:12-35 as you prepare.
Have your Bible open as you tell the story
to remind the children this Joseph is a real person from Scripture.
Retell the story in your own words or use the dialogue below

There is a map at the end of this lesson if you'd like to show the children
how far Joseph traveled to find his brothers and eventually get to Egypt.

Jacob and his sons took care of sheep. Do you know what you call a whole bunch of sheep? *(Allow for answers.)* A group of sheep is called a flock. Jacob and his sons had more sheep than you can count, the Bible says they had many flocks. So they moved the sheep from field to field to make sure had enough grass to eat. Sometimes they had to go far from home to find grass for their flocks.

Once when the ten older brothers had been gone for a while with the sheep, Jacob sent Joseph to check on them. Joseph walked about fifty miles to find his brothers. How long do you think it would take to walk that far? *(Allow for answers)* Joseph would have walked about two days to find them. But when he got to the place they were supposed to be, his brothers were gone! So Joseph kept looking.

Finally, after walking one more day, Joseph spotted the flocks in the distance. And that's when Joseph's brothers saw him coming.

Do you know what Joseph's brothers did? *(Allow for answers.)* Do you think they ran out to greet him and gave him big hugs? *(Allow for answers.)* Maybe they talked about how much they missed him. What do you think? *(Allow for answers)* No way!

Joseph's brothers started plotting against him. They wanted to get rid of him. His brothers decided they would throw him in a well, a deep hole with water, and tell their father he was eaten by a lion or a tiger.

Now, Joseph's oldest brother, Reuben, didn't want to see Joseph drown, but he also didn't want to go against all the other brothers. He convinced them to put him in a dry well so he wouldn't drown. So they took Joseph's beautiful coat off of him and put him in a deep dark hole. Reuben planned to come back when the other brothers weren't looking and rescue Joseph. But before Reuben could save him, something else happened. Can you guess? *(Allow for answers.)*

While Reuben was away from camp, probably taking his turn watching the sheep, the other brothers sat down to eat. During dinner a caravan passed by. Do you know what a caravan is? *(Allow for answers)* A caravan consists of many camels and wagons and lots of people walking, all heading to the same place. It was a safer way to travel. The caravan gave Joseph's brother, Judah, an idea. He said, "Let's sell Joseph. The people in this caravan will buy him. He'll be a slave, but at least he'll be alive." So they did.

When Reuben came back, he was shocked. They ruined his plan. He couldn't believe they'd sold his brother! What would they tell their father?

To cover up their horrible deed, they took Joseph's robe, dipped it in the blood of a sheep and told their father they'd found it in the desert. They convinced Jacob a wild animal had killed his favorite son.

Jacob cried for many days. He said he would never get over losing Joseph.

But we know something Jacob didn't. Was Joseph really dead? *(Allow for answers)* No! Joseph traveled many, many miles to Egypt. Next week we'll talk about what happened to Joseph in Egypt.

HELPING THEM REMEMBER

MEMORY VERSE   5 Minutes
Matthew 5:44

Love your enemies ♦ and pray for those ♦ who mistreat you ♦ Matthew 5:44

DO: Say the verse several times breaking at the ♦ and allowing students to repeat. After they know it fairly well:

SAY: Who are your enemies? *(Allow for answers.)*

Does anyone mistreat you? *(Allow for answers.)*

How does Jesus say we should treat them? *(Allow for answers. Encourage students to say love them and pray for them)*

Can you love your enemies and pray for people who treat you badly? *(Allow for answers)*

We can only do it with God's help, so let's stop and pray. We will ask Jesus to help us love people who aren't very loveable. *(Encourage children to close their eyes and fold*

Dear Jesus,

Loving people who treat us badly is difficult. But we know we can do it with your help. So right now we pray for our enemies. Bless them, Lord, and help them see how much you love them so they won't have to bully others. Teach us to love like you love. In Your Holy Name we pray, Amen.

ACTIVITY   5-10 Minutes

Am I a Bully?

Materials Needed: Scrap Paper (at least half sheets of paper), White board, Pencils

SAY: We want to make sure we are never bullies like Joseph's brothers. So today we're going to write down some words to describe bullies.

DO: Give each child six of more pieces of scrap paper. Help them write or draw pictures to describe the actions of bullies and the names they use to belittle others. Remind them not to write names of real people, just names they call others. You might write the ideas on a white board so the children can copy. Encourage young ones to draw pictures that represent the words. Include the things Joseph's brothers did. Ask kids what others call them. Refrain from giving them ideas of names to call others. Ideas from Joseph's life: Dreamer, They are mean, Drop in a well, Sell to strangers, Hurt others, Call names, Steal things, Make me feel bad, etc.

SAY: How does it make you feel when others treat you badly? *(Allow for answers)*
Do you ever treat anyone like this? *(Allow for answers)*
Do you ever call people names, even your brothers or sisters? *(Allow for answers)*
How do you think that makes them feel? *(Allow for answers)*

Jesus doesn't want us to be like Joseph's brothers. He asks us to treat other people like we want to be treated.

So what do you do when others treat you badly? *(Allow for answers.)*
It's hard not to cry or to be mean in return, but today we're going to play a game to help us remember what to do when others treat us poorly.

GAME   5-10 Minutes

Throw Away the Bad Names

Materials Needed: Paper from the activity and masking/painters tape

DO: Before class put a piece of tape on the floor about six feet long in the middle of the space where you'll play the game. Then divide the children into two teams. Make sure the older children are divided somewhat evenly between the teams. You can play this game with only two children if necessary!

SAY: When people say mean things, sometimes the best thing we can do is let it go and forget about it. Things bullies say are never true. We also need to remember to never say mean things to others. We want to get rid of all those mean words so we're never bullies like Joseph's brothers. Those mean things are so unimportant we're going to wad them up in balls. *(Demonstrate wadding up one of the pieces of scrap paper with the names on it and encourage children to wad their scraps)*

To play our game each team will be on one side of this piece of tape. *(Show the tape you placed on the floor earlier)*

When I say go, you'll start throwing away all of these bad names and hurtful actions. We're going to get rid of them. They aren't important, and we don't want to use these words to hurt others.

You will throw them to the other team's side of the tape. Which means you'll keep getting more pieces of paper. But sometimes that's how bullies work. Even when you try to ignore them, they keep giving you more.

Your goal today is to get all of the paper on the other team's side of the tape.

DO: Say go when you're ready. Allow the children to throw the paper for as long as you have time. If one team manages to clear their side, declare them the winner; however, that probably won't happen. So when it's time to end the game:

SAY: Neither team managed to get rid of all the hurtful names. But that's how it is in real life. It's important we remember not to be a bully and not to retaliate, because when we try to get back at others it never ends. We can only end the meanness by practicing our memory verse. What did it say? *(Allow for answers. Then repeat it with the class a couple of times.)*

CRAFT   10-15 Minutes

Love Your Enemies Bracelet

Materials Needed: Plastic Lacing Cord one 12" piece per student, four Heart Beads, one Black Pony Beads and Two White Pony Beads per student.

DO: Pass out the lacing cord and beads

SAY: Today we're going to make a bracelet to remind us to love and forgive our enemies.

1. First put a heart bead on your lace to remind you to love.

2. Then put a white bead to remind you to forgive. Forgiveness makes us white and clean like Jesus.

3. Next we're going to add another heart bead. What will it remind us of? *(Allow for answers.)* Right! Jesus tells us to love.

4. Who did Jesus tell us to love? *(Allow for answers.)* Our enemies. The black bead will go next to remind us of our enemies.

5. But we'll put another heart bead next so our enemy is surrounded by love.

6. Next let's add another white bead. What did the white bead remind us of? *(Allow for answers)* Forgiveness. When we forgive we are NOT telling them it's OK. We're just getting rid of the anger and the names. We're choosing to not hang on to it, like we did the wads of paper.

7. Then we'll end with another heart. Why? *(Allow for answers)* We always want to end with love because Jesus loves us so much!

CLOSING MOMENTS
Clean Up and Prayer Time

Encourage the children to clean up their ministry space. Make sure they push in chairs and pick up all the extra beads and garbage. Gather them in a circle and then close with the prayer below or pray spontaneously.

Dear Jesus,

We praise you because you are our friend. Lord, we don't ever want to be mean like Joseph's brothers. Help us to always treat others with love, even our enemies. Remind us to throw off bad names and pray for those who call us those names. Thank you that you always love us. In Your Holy Name we pray, Amen

Map of Joseph's Search for his Brothers and His Trip to Egypt

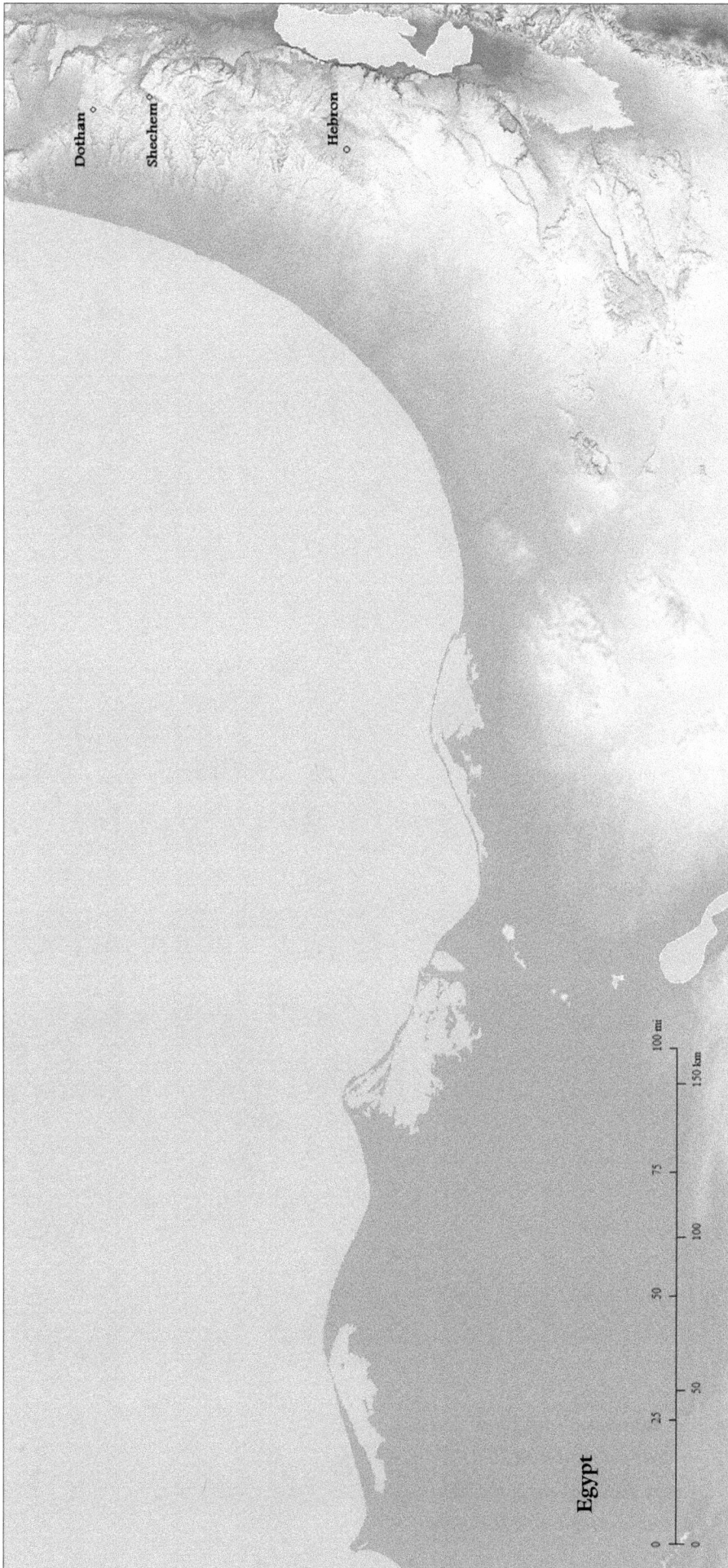

Dothan ◇

Shechem ◇

Hebron ○

Egypt

100 mi

150 km

75

100

50

50

25

25

0

0

Joseph lived in Hebron. He travelled to Shechem to find his brothers, but when they weren't there, he found them in Dothan.

Then the caravan took him to Egypt.

Intentionally left blank
so if you print from PDF
or tear the lesson out of the book
the next lesson falls on a fresh page

The Life of Joseph

Lesson Four: Being Trustworthy and Living Blessed

INTRODUCTION/LEADER'S DEVOTION

When Joseph arrived in Egypt, the Ishmaelites sold him to Potiphar, one of Pharaoh's officials. Joseph quickly became head of all the servants. His faithfulness to God brought him blessings, and Joseph prospered even as a slave. His blessed living got Potiphar's attention. So Pharaoh's official trusted Joseph with everything in his house, confident the young Hebrew slave would take care of it.

Can we be trusted like Joseph? When you say you're going to do something, do you get it done? Do your friends know when you borrow their possessions, they'll come back as good as or better than you received them?

Teaching the kids about being trustworthy may be one of the most important lessons they'll learn in this era. Compromising has shoved integrity to the wayside. This week we'll help the children see the importance of being trusted and the blessings of being a child of God.

OVERVIEW

OPENING ACTIVITY   5 Minutes

Who Can You Trust?

Materials: Copy of the last page of this lesson on Cardstock or Photo Paper with images cut apart.

BIBLE LESSON   10 Minutes

Genesis 39:1-6

HELPING THEM REMEMBER

ACTIVITY   5-10 Minutes

Build a Trust Wall

Materials Needed: About 40 boxes that are all about the same size (cereal or tissue boxes would work well)

MEMORY VERSE   5 Minutes

Proverbs 12:22

Continue with the Trust Wall

CRAFT   10-20 Minutes

Special Agent Pin

Materials Needed: Felt, Construction Paper, Safety Pins or Butterfly Craft Pins, Markers, Glue, Pattern from next page OPTIONAL: Small foam cross stickers

GAME   5-10 Minutes

Collect the Trust

Supplies: Colored discs (wood coins, plastic chips, etc) in two or three colors, Sharpie, basket

CLOSING MOMENTS   5 Minutes

Clean Up and Prayer Time

The Life of Joseph - Lesson Four:
Being Trustworthy and Living Blessed

OPENING ACTIVITY   5 Minutes

Who Can You Trust?

Materials: Copy of the last page of this lesson on Cardstock or Photo Paper with images cut apart.

DO: Show the children each of the pictures from the last page. If you have more than 10 children, you may want two sets.

SAY: If you had $10, which of these people would you trust to hold it for you? *(Allow each of the children to pick one. They may all choose the same photo.)* Why did you choose this person? *(Allow for answers.)*

(Show the pictures of the service man and the police officers) We should usually be able to trust police officers and service men. So, these two were good choices.

(Show the picture of the mom) Moms are usually good choices to trust. So, if you picked this person to hold your $10 it would probably be safe.

(Show the picture of the handcuffs - presumably no one picked this) Why didn't you choose this picture? *(Allow for answers)* You are correct, generally people in handcuffs have been in trouble before and need to prove themselves before we trust them.

(Show the picture of the little girl and the old man. If anyone chose one of these mention that and ask the rest of the group:) Why didn't you choose the young girl or the old man? *(Allow for answers)* We don't know enough about these two to know whether or not they're trustworthy, do we? Even with the soldier, the mom and the policemen, we'd be taking a chance. But with these two we need more information. Trust is something you earn. Policemen, soldiers and moms have earned it because other moms and people in uniform have proven to be trustworthy. But just one bad policeman, soldier or mom can make it hard to trust the next one.

Would anyone trust YOU with their $10? *(Allow for answers)*

Today Joseph will teach us how to earn trust.

BIBLE LESSON   10 Minutes

Genesis 39:1-6

Have your Bible open as you tell the story
to remind the children this Joseph is a real person from Scripture.
Retell the story in your own words or use the dialogue below

Let's review what we know about Joseph so far. What can you tell me? *(Allow for answers. Affirm answers from the list below and fill in where the children miss)*

- Joseph was Jacob's (aka Israel) favorite.

- He had ten older brothers.

- Because he was the favorite, his dad gave him a fancy coat.

- He had two dreams about stars and wheat bowing down to him.

- His brothers were jealous so they threw him in a pit and took his fancy coat.

- His brothers sold him to some traveling salesmen (Ishmaelites) passing by

- The Ishmaelite *(pronounced ish-male-ite)* travelers took Joseph to Egypt. *(You could show the map on Page 22 to demonstrate how far Joseph traveled)*

Today we're going to learn about Joseph's first days in this new country.

When they arrived in Egypt, the Ishmaelites sold Joseph to a man named Potiphar. Potiphar was an important man in Egypt. He was in charge of the soldiers who guarded Pharaoh, the King of Egypt. So Joseph became a slave. How do you think it would feel to be a slave in Egypt? *(Allow for answers)* What kinds of things do slaves have to do? *(Allow for answers, but let them know slaves have to do everything they're told and can be beaten when they disobey)*

What would you do if you were a slave? *(Allow for answers)* Most people would try to escape or cheat their master. But Joseph trusted God, so he was different. Joseph knew God would take care of him, so he did things to honor God, and God blessed his work. Because He trusted and obeyed God, good things happened to Joseph even though life didn't seem very good.

It didn't take long for Potiphar to notice that everything Joseph did turned out well. The Bible said Joseph had success in everything he did. Potiphar noticed God was blessing Joseph, so he gave Joseph a slave promotion. Potiphar put Joseph in charge of all the other slaves. In fact Joseph took care of Potiphar's entire house.

Potiphar put him in control of all his money and his food. He trusted Joseph to take care of everything because Joseph proved he could be trusted. And because Joseph trusted and obeyed God, God kept blessing Joseph. God had a hand in everything Joseph did. God blessed all of his work.

So, Potiphar's fields produced more crops, and he got more money. With Joseph in charge, everything Potiphar owned got bigger and all his plans succeeded because God was blessing Joseph. Potiphar trusted Joseph, and Joseph had the best life a slave could have.

HELPING THEM REMEMBER

ACTIVITY 5-10 Minutes

Build a Trust Wall
Materials Needed: About 40 boxes that are all about the same size (cereal or tissue boxes would work well)

1. Lay down the first row of boxes (about 8)

2. Ask the children, "What about you makes you a good friend" When they tell you, give them a box. *(Don't let them use physical qualities)* OPTION: Use a Sharpie to write the quality on the side of the box

3. Have kids put their box on the stack centering it over two boxes in the previous row. Put seven in the second row and one less in each subsequent row. Encourage the children to place them carefully so none of the boxes fall. If you have a small group, you could allow each child to name two or three qualities. You could also name extra

qualities and write them on the boxes and allow the children to add the boxes to the wall.

Ideas for qualities to write on the boxes: I share, I'm truthful, don't lie, loyal, trustworthy, friendly, helpful, nice, caring, dependable, adventurous, giver, positive, accepting, forgiving, supportive, loving, funny, understanding, patient, cheerful, considerate, generous, kind, good listener, sincere, dependable, polite, like to play, not selfish, positive, easy going, works hard, hugs good, gives gifts, doesn't bully, like to talk, sympathetic, patient, like to laugh, don't gossip

SAY: When we act trustworthy and obedient to God, it's like we're building a sturdy wall. Our integrity makes us strong and pleases God. - *Then move to the Memory Verse*

MEMORY VERSE   5 Minutes
Proverbs 12:22

God hates lying lips, ◆ but delights in those ◆ who are trustworthy ◆ Proverbs 12:22

SAY: Joseph obeyed God. He was trustworthy, so God blessed him. Joseph had the qualities we put in our Trust Wall. These qualities make us strong like a wall. There's a verse in Proverbs to help us remember to be like Joseph. *(Say the Memory verse a few times breaking it into three parts so the children can repeat after you)*

What does this verse say about lying? *(Allow for answers.)* Proverbs says God hates lying lips. So let's take out our truthful block, because according to God, we can't trust someone who lies.

(Pick five or six people to carefully take out one block each) Each of you will take out one block from our trust wall. *(Give assistance where needed so the wall doesn't topple).* What happens to our wall when these blocks are missing? *(Allow for answers)* Every time we remove a block our wall gets weaker. And when we are missing these traits we become weak. In order to be a good friend, to be strong and trustworthy, we need all these traits.

CRAFT   10-20 Minutes
Special Agent Pin
Materials Needed: Felt, Construction Paper, Safety Pins or Butterfly Craft Pins, Markers, Glue, Pattern from next page OPTIONAL: Small foam cross stickers

Use the instructions on the pattern page to create Special Agent Pins

SAY: Potiphar trusted Joseph because Joseph followed God. When we act like Jesus we become trustworthy too! You can wear this badge as a reminder that we should follow God and be like Joseph, honest and trustworthy.

GAME   5-10 Minutes
Collect the Trust
Supplies: Colored discs (wood coins, plastic chips, etc) in two or three colors, Sharpie, basket

PREPARE: Before class, write all of the positive traits you wrote on the boxes on discs. Make these all one or two colors for your non-readers. On a different color write about 10-20 traits that are opposite of those we wrote on the boxes (ie: liar, cheat, thief, etc) Then hide them around your ministry area before class begins

SAY: Hidden around the room are discs with trustworthy traits on them, but there are also a bunch of traits we don't want to have. The trustworthy traits are all on *(tell them what color you used for your trustworthy traits)*. You have a few minutes to find and collect as many trustworthy traits as you can. When you find the untrustworthy traits, you should drop them in my basket. Let's see who can find the most trustworthy traits!

DO*:* Give the students as much time as you have to find the discs. You could keep track of which students put the untrustworthy traits in your basket. If you do, make a big deal about the person who threw away the most unwanted traits. Help the kids understand getting rid of bad habits is just as important as gaining good ones.

SAY: How many did each of you collect? *(Allow for answers. If you want to give a prize to the one who found the most, you may.)* Collecting trustworthy traits is important. Let's name some of these traits we found. *(Allow older children to read the traits or accept any correct answer.)* How many of these traits have you collected in your life? Are you honest? Do you treat friends with respect? *(Allow children to answer.)* We had fun collecting these discs, but it's even more important to collect traits in real life, to be a good friend, to be like Joseph.

CLOSING MOMENTS   5 Minutes

Clean Up and Prayer Time

Encourage the children to clean up their ministry space. Make sure they push in chairs and pick up garbage. Gather them in a circle and close with the prayer below or pray spontaneously.

Dear Jesus,

We praise you because you are our friend. We can always trust you! Help us to be like Joseph so others can always trust us too! In Your Holy Name we pray, Amen.

Cut one of these out of felt for each student
Cut on the dark black line

Also cut one from construction paper (or
tagboard or poster board.)

Cut a Small shield out of
Construction Paper for
each student.

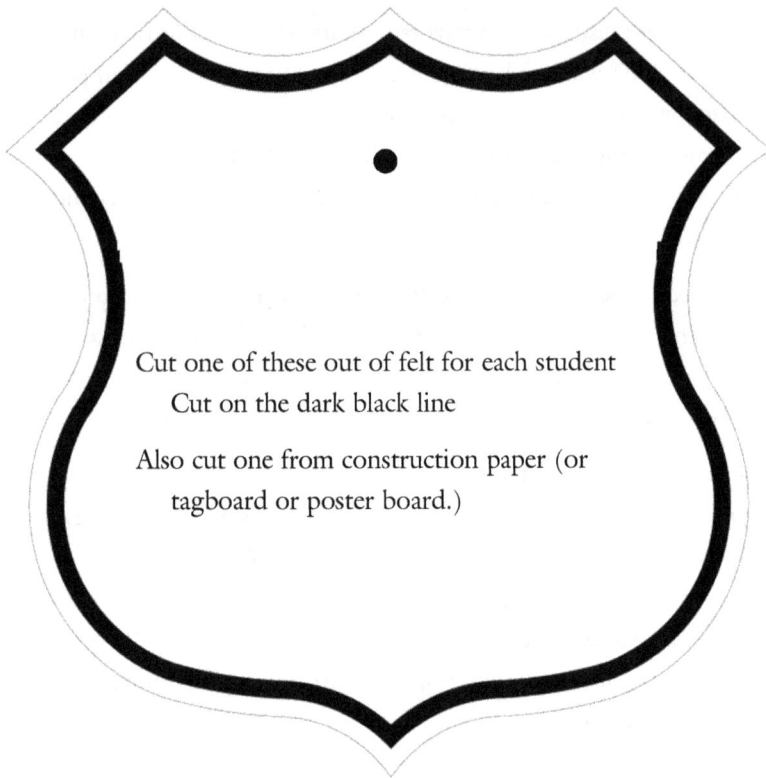

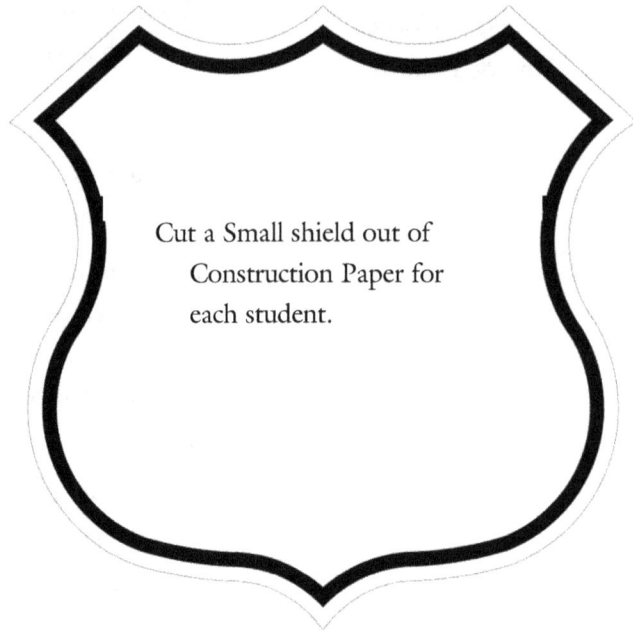

1. For Regular Pins Backs: On the back of the large construction paper shield (or tagboard), use duct tape to secure a safety pin. Then glue the felt to the front.

2. For Butterfly type pins: Glue the felt to the construction paper and stick the butterfly pin through the spot marked with a dot, so the flat part is against the felt. Attach the back so no one gets stuck.

3. On the small shield write: "God's Special Agent" OPT: put a small foam cross at the bottom center

4. Glue the small shield to the center of the large shield (covering the butterfly pin front if you used those).

5. Allow the glue to dry as you continue with the explanation of our shield.

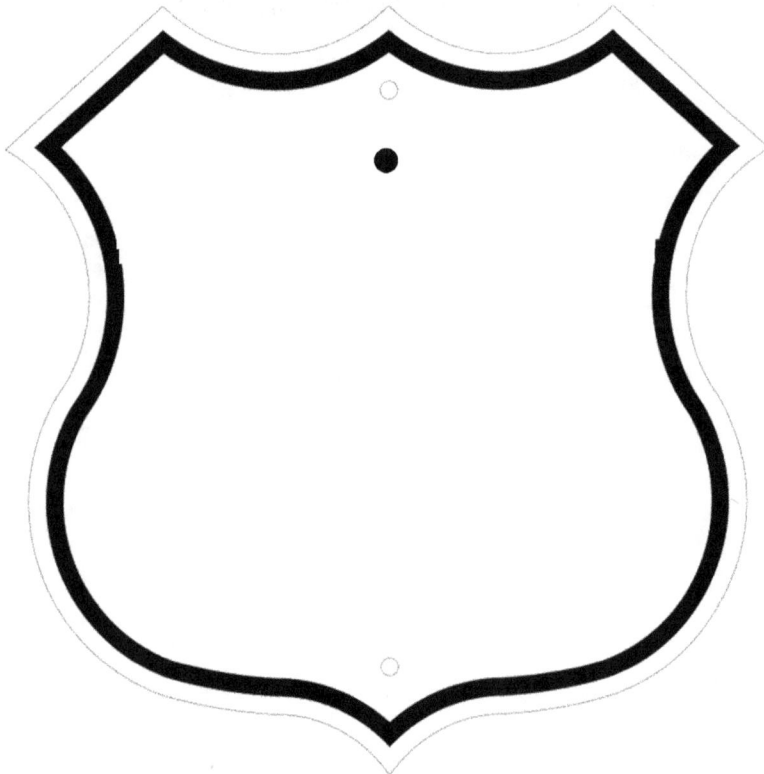

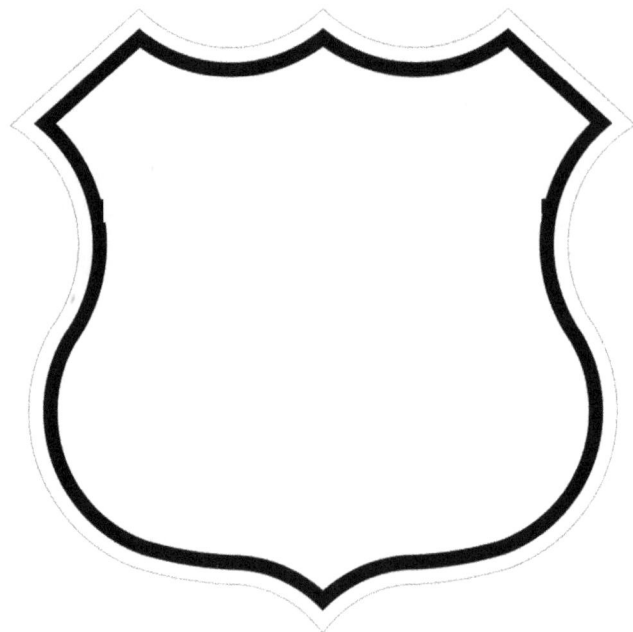

Make one copy
on Cardstock
and cut apart
for Opening

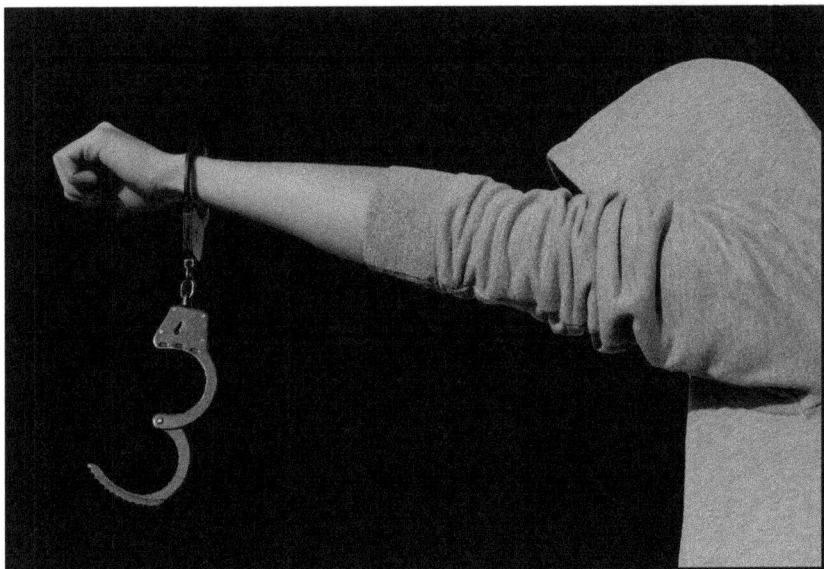

Intentionally left blank
so if you print from PDF
or tear the lesson out of the book
the next lesson falls on a fresh page

The Life of Joseph

Lesson Five: The Damage Caused by Lies

INTRODUCTION/LEADER'S DEVOTION

Just when everything seemed to going well for Joseph, life took a turn for the worse. An attractive young man, Joseph probably wasn't more than twenty when he rose to head servant in Potiphar's house. Yet, even in charge, he was still a slave, a fact Potiphar's wife thought she could use in her favor.

But when she tried to lure the young servant into her bed, Joseph's integrity won out. Joseph continued to do the right thing even though following his boss's wife would have made his life a lot easier, and maybe even more fun! Unfortunately, Potiphar's wife lacked any kind of scruples, so when Joseph refused her, she turned the tables and accused him of being the seductor.

We've all had people lie about us, and endured the unjust penalty of the tale. However, this women's lie landed Joseph in the dungeon for several years. For the second time Joseph went from being the favorite to the forgotten through no fault of his own.

Joseph's faith provides a great lesson for adults as well as children. Even when others lie, and our lives become damaged by those lies, God is still in control. He has a plan. Just wait for it.

OVERVIEW

OPENING ACTIVITY   5 Minutes
  Lies are Like Wooden Blocks
  Materials Needed: Wooden Blocks

BIBLE LESSON   10 Minutes
  Genesis 39:7-23

HELPING THEM REMEMBER

  MEMORY VERSE   5 Minutes
    Exodus 20:16

  GAME   5-10 Minutes
    Truth Destroys Lies
    Materials Needed: Wooden Blocks from Opening, White paper or Nerf balls

  CRAFT   10-20 Minutes
    Truth Bracelet
    Materials Needed: Elastic Cord, 9mm Pony beads, Square Letter Beads

  ACTIVITY   5-10 Minutes
    What about Truth?
    Materials Needed: Handout from last page

CLOSING MOMENTS   5 Minutes
  Clean Up and Prayer Time

The Life of Joseph - Lesson Five: The Damage Caused by Lies

OPENING ACTIVITY   5 Minutes

Lies are Like Wooden Blocks

Materials Needed: Wooden Blocks

DO: As you talk to the kids stack the blocks. Stack them straight up, not in a staggered form.

SAY: How many of you have played with wooden blocks? *(Allow for answers.)* What happens when you step on them? *(Allow for answers.)* They hurt my feet when I step on them. Do you ever throw your blocks? *(Allow for answers.)* What happens when you throw them? *(Keep pressing for answers until someone says, "Someone gets hurt." and/or "Things get broken")*

Lies are like wooden blocks. They hurt people and break friendships. Did you notice I've been stacking these as we talk? Lies are like that. After you tell a lie you need another lie to cover the first lie until eventually, the lies become a huge wall that keeps out our friends and God.

So, why do we lie? *(Allow for answers)* Lying always causes damage. Today we're going to hear how a lie nearly ruined Joseph's life.

BIBLE LESSON   10 Minutes

Genesis 39:6b-23

> *Have your Bible open as you tell the story*
> *to remind the children this Joseph is a real person from Scripture.*
> *Retell the story in your own words or use the dialogue below*

Let's review what we know about Joseph so far. What can you tell me? (Allow for answers. Affirm answers from the list below and fill in where the children miss)

- Joseph was Jacob's (aka Israel) favorite.

- He had ten older brothers.

- Because he was the favorite, his dad gave him a fancy coat.

- He had two dreams about stars and wheat bowing down to him.

- His brothers were jealous so they threw him in a pit and took his fancy coat.

- His brothers sold him to some traveling salesmen (Ishmaelites) passing by

- Joseph had great success because he was trustworthy and followed God

- Joseph had an important job in Potiphar's house.

Joseph grew into a very good-looking young man. He worked hard every day in Potiphar's house to make sure everything ran smoothly Potiphar didn't worry about a thing!

There was just one problem. Mrs. Potiphar noticed Joseph was handsome and had nice muscles. *(Make some muscles and invite the kids to show their muscles)* So Mrs. Potiphar started flirting with Joseph. Do you know what flirting is? *(Allow for answers)* Mrs. Potiphar started talking sweet to Joseph. She said all kinds of nice things and invited him for dinner when Potiphar was away on business. But Joseph knew that was wrong. Mrs. Potiphar was married to Potiphar and Joseph knew God made marriage special. So every time Mrs. Potiphar invited Joseph for dinner, Joseph turned her down. He told her, "Potiphar trusts me with everything in his house. He trusts me to take care of you. I could never break his trust and sin against God." But Mrs. Potiphar just kept inviting him.

Finally Mrs. Potiphar got very angry that Joseph kept telling her no. So she came up with a plan. One day when he was in the room with her taking care of things, she asked him one more time, but this time when he said no, she grabbed his long jacket and wouldn't let him leave. Joseph knew he had to get out of there so he slipped out of his jacket and left. Now Mrs. Potiphar could get even with him for turning her down everyday.

As Joseph was running out, Mrs. Potiphar screamed and the other servants hurried in. She told them that Joseph had started to undress in front of her and her scream had caused him to run off without his jacket. Was that the truth? (*Allow for answers*) No, Mrs. Potiphar lied!

Then when Potiphar got home, do you know what she did? (*Allow for answers*) She lied again! Mrs. Potiphar told him the same story. Do you remember the lie? (*Allow for answers*) Yes, she told Potiphar Joseph had started to undress in front of her and left his jacket when she screamed. And then she showed Potiphar the jacket as proof!

Potiphar was furious. He thought Joseph was trying to take his wife! He didn't even give Joseph a chance to tell his side of the story. He just took Joseph and put him in prison.

So Joseph went from living in a wonderful, comfy home to a place with dirt and mice. For the second time in his life Joseph was a prisoner and he hadn't done anything wrong either time.

How would you feel if that happened to you? (*Allow for answers*) Most people would be angry and get mad at God. But Joseph kept trusting God and doing his best, and God blessed him, even in prison. It didn't take long for the warden (the head prison guard) to notice that Joseph was trustworthy and God was with him. The warden put Joseph in charge of all the other prisoners, and Joseph could walk around without chains because he was taking care of everyone else.

God can bless us even when people try to cause damage with their lies.

HELPING THEM REMEMBER

MEMORY VERSE   5 Minutes

Exodus 20:16

Do not tell lies about your neighbor

Exodus 20:16

SAY: Who has heard of the Ten Commandments? (*Allow for answers*) What are some of those commands God gave us? (*Allow for answers - affirm each correct answer. If someone gives a "rule" that's not one of the Ten, let them know that's probably a good rule to follow, but not one of the Ten Commandments. Here's a reminder: No other Gods, No Idols, No misusing God's name, Holy Sabbath, Honor parents, No murder, No adultery, No Stealing, No Lies, No Coveting - Don't worry about covering them all. When someone mentions no lying:)* Yes, that commandment is our memory verse today.

DO: Have the children repeat the verse above a few times including chapter and verse. If you use a more difficult translation, be sure the children understand what "false testimony" is.

GAME   5-10 Minutes

Truth Destroys Lies
Materials Needed: Wooden Blocks from Opening, White paper crumbled into balls (or about 20 Nerf balls)

SAY: Do you remember our wooden blocks from before? What does each block represent? *(Allow for answers)* Each block represents one lie that was told. What would happen if I threw one of these blocks at one of you? *(Allow for answers)* These block could really hurt someone, but did you know lies hurt almost as bad? When you lie about someone you cause damage, just like these wooden blocks. Today we're going to play a game. Half of you will be the liars and half of you will be the truth tellers. Don't worry we'll let you change half way through. *(Show a sheet of white paper - revise the following text if you use Nerf balls)* These pieces of paper represent the truth. The truth is pure and clean. And while the truth can sometimes hurt a little, like a piece of paper can cause a paper cut, the truth can destroy lies.

DO: Divide the class into two groups with an equal number of older/younger kids on each team. If you haven't already done so, allow the children to crumple four or five sheets of paper each.

SAY: One team will try to build the lies and keep out the truth, while the other team tries to knock down the lies. The truth team will throw the truth balls at the block wall to knock them down. The liars team will keep rebuilding the wall and throw the truth balls back at the truth tellers. If the truth tellers knock down the whole wall or get all of their balls of truth on the other side of the wall, they win and we'll switch. *(At some point, the kids on the lying team may think to ask how they can win. If they do, tell them liars can never win, but they can see how long they can keep the truth tellers from winning. When the truth tellers win or half of your allotted time has passed, let the teams switch sides)*

CRAFT   10-20 Minutes

Truth Bracelet
Materials Needed: Elastic Cord, 9mm Pony beads, Square Letter Beads

DO: Give each child about 10" of elastic cord with one pony bead tied to the end of it. Allow them to pick out about ten pony beads of any color. Give each child the letter beads to spell TRUTH.

Have each one string five pony beads, then add TRUTH (make sure the bead that is tied on is to the left as they string, otherwise it will be spelled backwards), then add the last five pony beads. Help children try the bracelet to be sure they don't need an extra bead or two for larger wrists, then assist them in tying a good knot.

SAY: I hope these letter beads remind you of our blocks today. Remember that truth is stronger than a lie but the truth doesn't cause damage. Lies put Joseph in prison. Our lies cause damage too. We want to always tell the truth.

ACTIVITY   5-10 Minutes

What about Truth?

Materials Needed: Handout from last page

SAY: The truth can sometimes be a little scary. If you break something and no one is around, what would you tell your mom, grandma or grown-up when she sees it? *(Allow for answers)* Why would someone lie about something like that? *(Allow for answers)* Yes, no one likes to get in trouble. But if you lie, and then your grown-up finds out about it, what happens? *(Allow for answers)* Usually it's worse. Sometimes you get a bigger punishment for the lie than you'd have gotten for the broken thing.

The Bible has a lot to say about the truth. So let's take a minute and read some of the truth verses.

DO: Give every student a copy of the Bible Verses. *(These verses are paraphrased to make them easier for children to understand)* Allow the older kids to read a few out loud, stopping to make certain they understand what the verse means. Use as many as you have time for, then encourage the children to take the list home and read them with their parents.

CLOSING MOMENTS   5 Minutes

Clean Up and Prayer Time

Encourage the children to clean up their ministry space. Make sure they push in chairs and pick up garbage and stray pony beads. Gather them in a circle and close with the prayer below or pray spontaneously.

Dear Jesus,

We praise you because you are Truth. Help us when we're tempted to tell a lie, Jesus. Sometimes we're afraid to tell the truth, but we know the truth is always best. Help us to always tell the truth. In Your Holy Name we pray, Amen.

Bible Verses About Truth

Whoever lives by the truth, lives in the light.
John 3:21

The truth will set you free.
John 8:32

Jesus said, "I am the Way, the Truth, and the Life."
John 14:6

God's Word is Truth.
John 17:17

Love rejoices in the Truth.
1 Corinthians 13:6

Always Speak the Truth in Love.
Ephesians 4:15

Let us love, not with words or speech, but with actions and Truth.
1John 3:18

I love to hear my children are walking in the Truth.
3 John 1:4

Who gets to live with God? . . . The one who speaks the Truth from the heart.
Psalm 15:1-2

God is close to everyone who calls on Him in Truth.
Psalm 145:18

Truthful lips live forever.
Proverbs 12:19

Always speak the Truth to each other. . . And love Truth and Peace
Zechariah 8:16 & 19

The Life of Joseph

Lesson Six: Promises Forgotten

INTRODUCTION/LEADER'S DEVOTION

Broken promises hurt. I'm guessing you've experienced a few, perhaps a promise you made, and likely at least one made to you. Maybe the hurt you felt wasn't as life altering as the promise the cupbearer broke.

While in prison Joseph was put in charge of Pharaoh's baker and cupbearer. Who knows what they did to make the king angry, but we know they were in prison for "some time." Like Joseph, God gave both men dreams about their future. Only Joseph could interpret the dreams, and Joseph made it clear Yahweh gave the interpretation. The baker would go to his death in three days, but the cupbearer would be restored to his prestigious position. Grateful for Joseph's vision, he promised to help Joseph find freedom, but as soon as he left the cell, he forgot.

The cupbearer's story can remind children and adults the importance of keeping promises. Joseph sat in prison two years longer than necessary because Pharaoh's most trusted servant forgot. Let's praise God He never forgets and keep in mind the importance of a promise kept.

OPENING ACTIVITY   5 Minutes

Broken Eggs
Materials Needed: Two Raw Eggs, clear bowl

BIBLE LESSON   10 Minutes

Genesis 40:1-23

HELPING THEM REMEMBER

MEMORY VERSE   5 Minutes

Deuteronomy 4:31
Materials Needed: Yarn or Heavy String

GAME   5-10 Minutes

Egg Race
Materials Needed: Four (or more) hardboiled eggs (or a dozen fresh eggs) and 2 spoons

CRAFT   10-20 Minutes

Broken Egg Mosaic
Materials Needed: Cross Graphic from end of less on Card Stock (one per child), broken egg shells in paper cups, construction paper in various colors, glue and glue sticks.

ACTIVITY   5-10 Minutes

Coloring Sheets and a New Nursery Rhyme
Materials Needed: Coloring page at end of lesson and download a coloring page of Humpty Dumpty here:
http://getcolorings.com/humpty-dumpty-coloring-page#humpty-dumpty-coloring-page-32.jpg

CLOSING MOMENTS   5 Minutes

Clean Up and Prayer Time

The Life of Joseph - Lesson Six: Promises Forgotten

OPENING ACTIVITY   5 Minutes

Broken Eggs

Materials Needed: Two Raw Eggs, clear bowl

As you begin, hold up the eggs and

SAY: What are these? *(Allow for answers.)* How do you use them? *(Allow for answers.)* What's the biggest concern with eggs? *(Allow for answers. You want them to say "breaking them.")* How many of you are afraid you'll break an egg? *(Allow for answers.)* What happens when we break them? *(Allow for answers)*

DO: Break one egg in the bowl. Try to make it look easy. You may want to avoid farm fresh eggs from yards that feed chickens a lot of shells and scratch, the shells will be harder.

SAY: Do you know how long this unbroken egg will last? *(Show the unbroken egg)* This egg in it's shell might last a month or more. Do you know how long the broken egg will last? *(Allow for answers.)* This egg will only last a few days. If we don't cook and eat this egg, it's ruined. And what would happen if I accidentally dropped it? *(Allow for answers.)* You're right, it would make a huge mess.

But do you know what else makes a huge mess when it's broken? *(Allow for answers. Expect answers like cups and trinkets.)* There's something that makes a bigger mess because it's harder to clean up. And that's a promise that's been broken. Today we're going to learn how Joseph handled a broken promise.

BIBLE LESSON   10 Minutes

Genesis 40:1-23

Have your Bible open as you tell the story
to remind the children this Joseph is a real person from Scripture.
Retell the story in your own words or use the dialogue below

Take a few moments to review what we know about Joseph's life so far:

- *Jacob's favorite son who got a beautiful coat*

- *Brothers were jealous and sold him into slavery*

- *Worked in Potiphar's house and rose to head servant*

- *Potiphar's wife lied about Joseph and Potiphar sent him to prison*

- *The prison guard trusted Joseph and put him in charge of the prison.*

So now Joseph is in prison. He is in charge of all the other prisoners, but regardless he's still in jail. Joseph spent several years in prison, then one day two of Pharaoh's top men ended up in there too. The chief baker and the chief cupbearer both made Pharaoh angry, and he sent them to the house of the captain of the guard.

What do you think the chief baker does? *(Allow for answers.)* That's pretty easy. He bakes for Pharaoh. He baked bread and cakes for every meal. What about the chief cupbearer? *(Allow for answers.)* The cupbearer was the most trusted person in the kingdom. He brought Pharaoh's wine and made certain no one had poisoned it. He often tasted the wine to test it for Pharaoh. We don't know what these two guys did, but something caused Pharaoh to become so angry he sent them to the prison where Joseph was in charge.

Joseph and Pharaoh's officials spent a good bit of time in prison. Then one night the cupbearer and the baker both had dreams. Both men were sad the next day because they were sure their dreams meant something, but they couldn't figure it out. When Joseph came in, he noticed their faces and asked them why they were sad.

They said, "We both had dreams, but no one can tell us what they mean?" So, how do you think Joseph answered them? *(Allow for answers.)*

Joseph said, "Only God can tell us what dreams mean. So tell me your dream." Did you notice who Joseph gave the credit to? *(Allow for answers.)* Joseph always gave God credit.

The cupbearer told his dream first. He'd seen a vine in his dream. It had three branches and it grew some very nice grapes. The cupbearer saw the good grapes, and in his dream he picked them and squeezed them into Pharaoh's cup and gave it to Pharaoh to drink.

Joseph said, "God told me what your dream means. The three branches mean three days. In three days you're going to get out of this prison. You'll be right back there with Pharaoh handing him his cup again. But when you're back in Pharaoh's house, please remember me. I shouldn't be here. I was wrongly sold and then someone told lies to put me here. So be sure to tell Pharaoh about me and get me out of here." The cupbearer agreed.

The baker heard the cupbearer's dream and thought his dream might mean the same thing. So he told Joseph his dream. The baker had seen three baskets of bread in his dream. The baskets were stacked on his head. The top basket had some of the best bread for Pharaoh, but the birds kept eating the bread from his baskets.

Then Joseph told the baker the bad news. The three baskets meant three days, too. But in three days Pharaoh would take him out of prison and kill him for his crime.

Three days later Pharaoh celebrated his birthday. He threw himself a big party and invited the chief cupbearer to return to his position. But the chief baker was killed just like Joseph had said.

The cupbearer had promised to help get Joseph out of prison. How long do you think it took the cupbearer to tell Pharaoh about Joseph? *(Allow for answers.)* The cupbearer was so happy, he got busy doing his job right away. He forgot all about Joseph. Joseph waited and waited, but no one came to get him out. The cupbearer forgot his promise.

HELPING THEM REMEMBER

MEMORY VERSE   5 Minutes
Deuteronomy 4:31
Materials Needed: Yarn or Heavy String

> *God is merciful; he will never forget you.*
> *Deuteronomy 4:31*

Repeat the verse with the children several times then:

SAY: God never forgets you, and He never forgets His promises. The cupbearer forgot the promise he made to Joseph. It's easy to forget. A long time ago people used to tie strings on their finger if they had something important to remember. So today we're going to try that! Hopefully these strings will help us remember our memory verse and remind us to always keep our promises.

DO: Tie a string loosely around one finger on each child. A few times during the activities ask them if they remember what the string is for.

GAME   5-10 Minutes

Egg Race

Materials Needed: Four (or more) hardboiled eggs (or a dozen fresh eggs), masking tape and 2 spoons

1. Use the masking tape to make a start and finish line about 10 feet apart.

2. Divide the group into two teams evenly distributing older and younger children.

3. Have the children line up behind the start line. Give the first student in each line a spoon and give them instructions.
    -- Each team will have an egg in their spoon. The first person will walk to the finish line and back without touching or dropping the egg. If the egg falls the person has to return to start and begin again.
    -- When the person gets back to the team line, they will hand off the egg and spoon to the next person. They may touch the egg to pass it off.
    -- The second person will repeat the process. The first team to get all the people to the finish line and back wins.

4. Put an egg on each spoon and begin. If you use raw eggs, you'll probably have to swap eggs a few times and clean up the mess so no one falls. If you use hard boiled, allow them to use the same egg until it becomes too damaged from the falls.

5. At the end gather the children and show them the eggs (or shells)

SAY: What happened when we dropped the eggs? *(Allow for answers.)* When we break promises or forget our friends, it's a lot like broken eggs. Have you ever had a friend forget about you? *(Allow for answers.)* It hurts when people forget us. It's important that we always keep our promises and remember to include our friends so they don't end up looking like these eggs!

CRAFT   10-20 Minutes

Broken Egg Mosaic

Materials Needed: Cross Graphic from end of lesson on Card Stock (one per child), broken egg shells in paper cups, construction paper in various colors, glue and glue sticks.

DO: Give each child a cross outline, scraps of construction paper and a cup of eggshells. Encourage them to tear the construction paper into small pieces (about 1/2") and cover the cross with them leaving space for some egg shells. (Glue sticks should work for the construction paper)

Then have them fill in with the eggs shells, they can cover some of the construction paper if they like. (If you have enough egg shells, you can omit the construction paper)

SAY: Do you remember our memory verse today? *(Allow for answers)* God never forgets us. And God always keeps His promises. God promised to send a Savior, and He did. God sent Jesus to die on the Cross for us to pay the price for our sin so we can be God's friend again. I hope the broken shells on this Cross remind you not only to keep your promises, but also that God always keeps His promises. He will never forget you!

ACTIVITY   5-10 Minutes

Creativity Sheet, Coloring Page and New Nursery Rhyme
Materials Needed: Copies of creativity sheet and coloring page at the end of this lesson (You could substitute this coloring page for the creativity sheet—http://getcolorings.com/humpty-dumpty-coloring-page)

DO: Pass out the coloring sheet with the grapes and bread. Encourage kids to color while you chat about the lesson.

SAY: What do these pictures remind you of? *(Allow for answers.)* What did the baker and the cupbearer dream? *(Allow for answers.)* What did Joseph tell them the dreams meant? *(Allow for answers.)* Which man made Joseph a promise? *(Allow for answers.)* What did he promise? *(Allow for answers.)* Did he keep his promise? *(Allow for answers.)* Keeping promises is important. Joseph stayed in prison a long time because of a broken promise.

DO: Pass out the Humpty Dumpty creativity sheet and ask kids to draw a picture of Humpty Dumpty and his wall.

SAY: Who knows the "Humpty Dumpty" rhyme? *(Encourage kids to say the rhyme)*
Humpty Dumpty sat on a wall, Humpty Dumpty had a great fall
All the King's horses and all the King's men couldn't put Humpty together again.

Now we're going to say the rhyme so it will remind us to keep our promises.
The promise I made sat on a wall, The promise I made had a great fall
Not one of the sorry's I said to my friends could put my promise together again

Remember, our promises are like eggs. Once we break them, we can't put them together. We must be like Jesus and always keep our promises.

DO: Repeat the rhyme several times. If you have time allow the children to color their creation or send the page home with them with the new rhyme on the bottom for them to remember.

CLOSING MOMENTS   5 Minutes

Clean Up and Prayer Time

Encourage the children to clean up their ministry space and then close with the prayer below or pray spontaneously.

Awesome God,

Thank you that you never forget me. We are so grateful for your promises, especially the promise of Jesus. Help us to never make phony promises and let your Spirit help us remember every promise we make. We want to be more like you every day.

In Jesus' precious Name, Amen

The Cross: God's Best Kept Promise

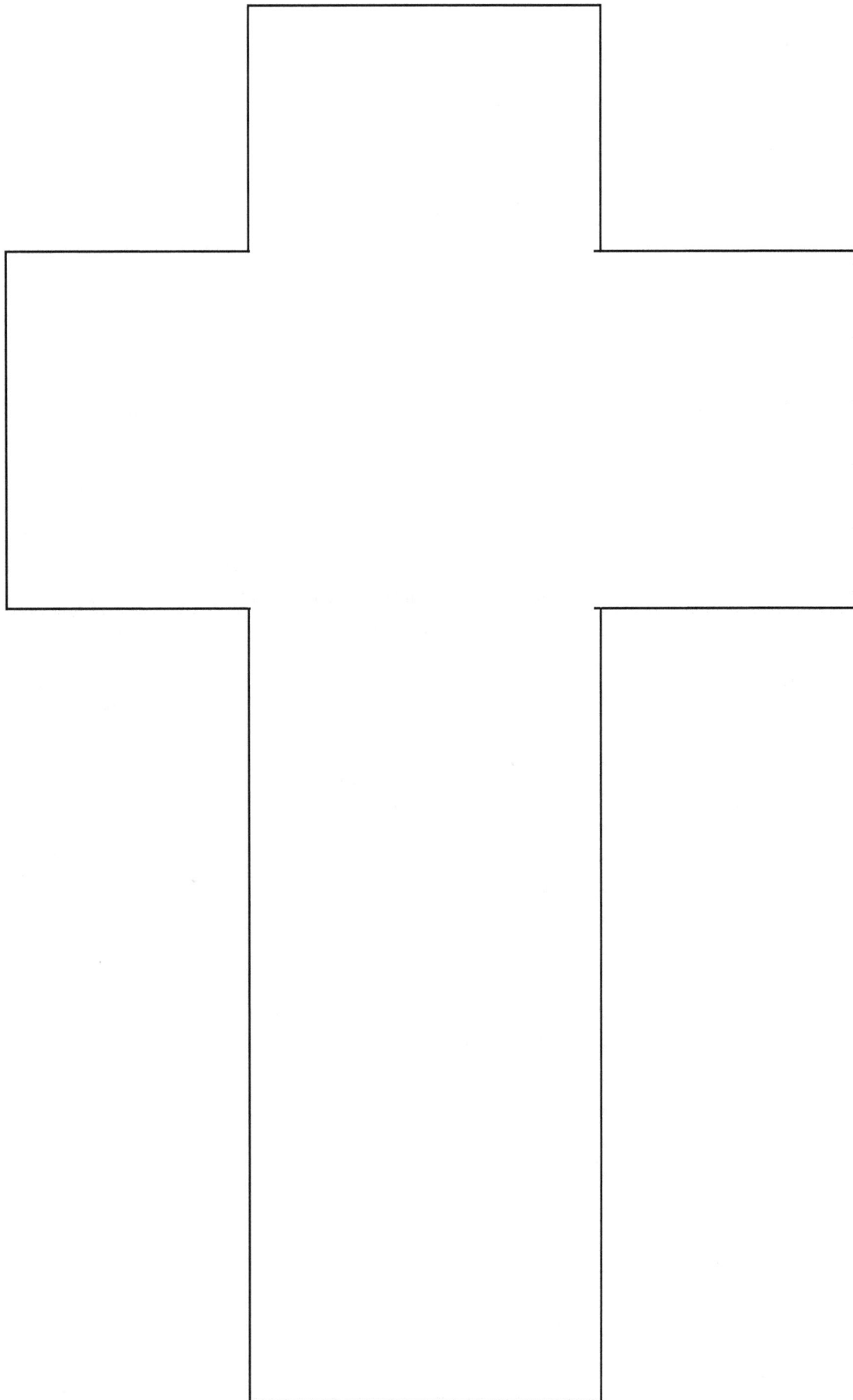

**Humpty Dumpty
reminds us
Broken Promises
can't be put
together again**

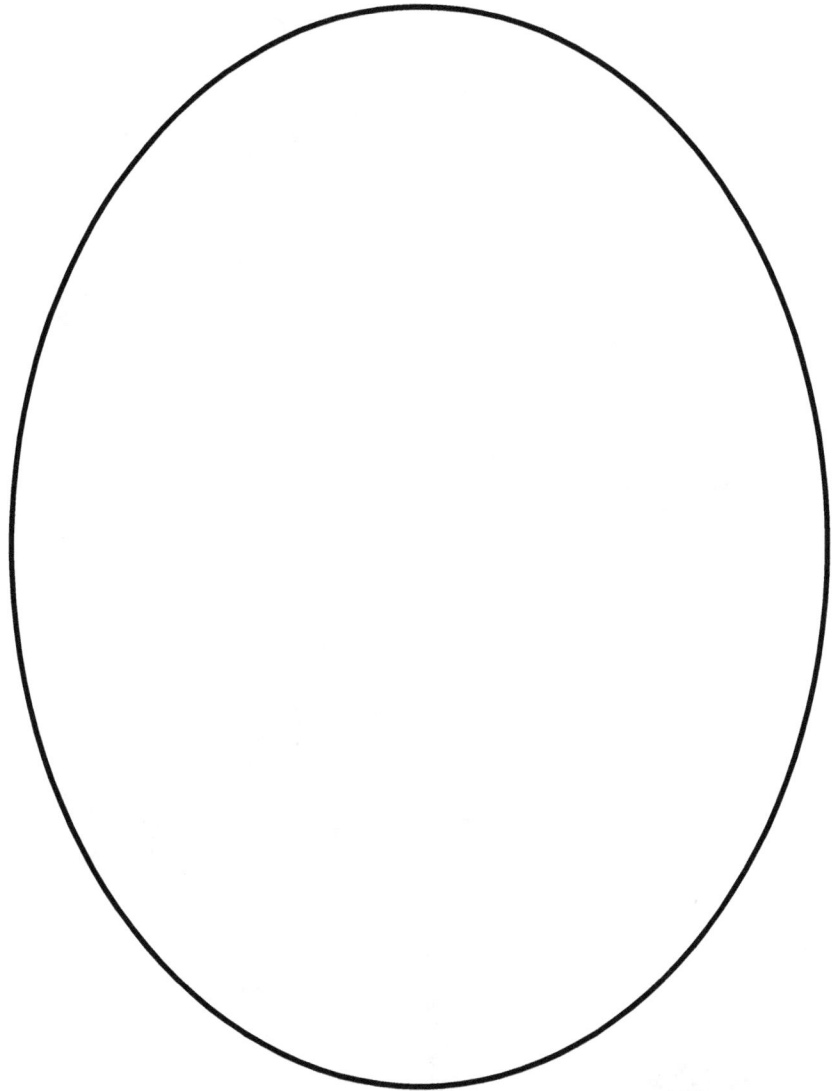

The promise I made sat on a wall,
The promise I made had a great fall
Not one of the sorry's I said to my friends
could put my promise together again.

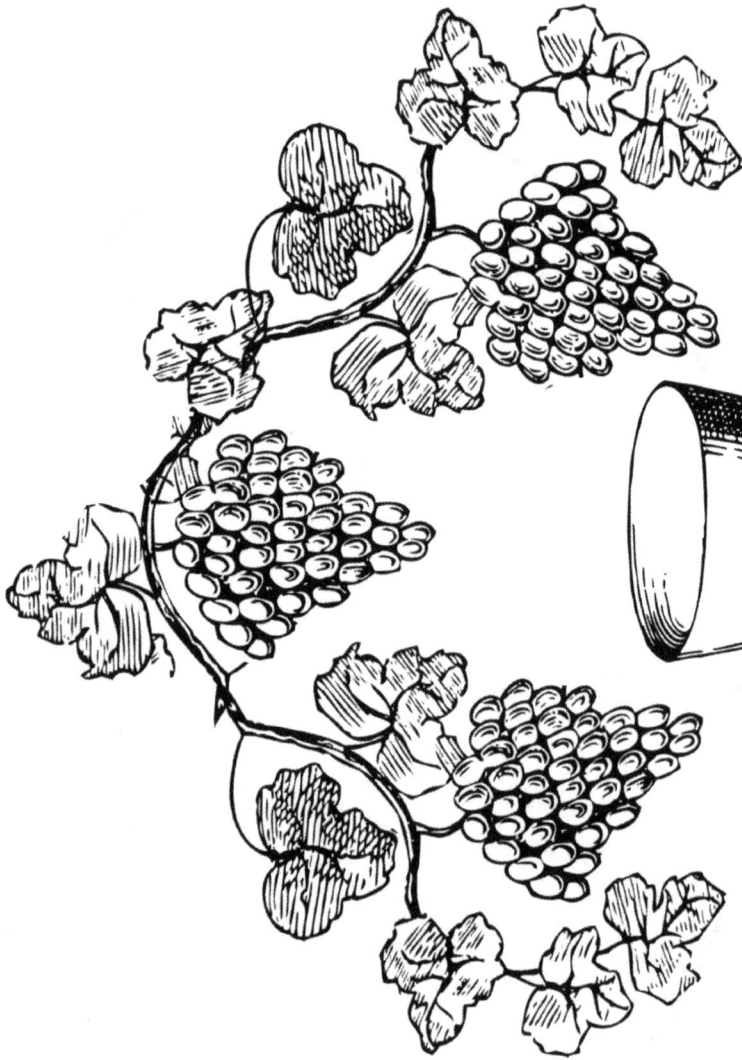

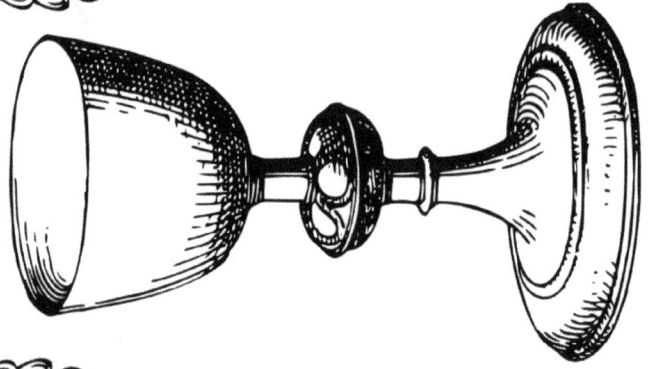

The Life of Joseph

Lesson Seven: God Never Leaves Us Alone

INTRODUCTION/LEADER'S DEVOTION

Joseph's story boasts one more dream, and it belonged to Pharaoh. Two years passed, and the cupbearer had completely forgotten about Joseph. Perhaps his forgetfulness sprang from convenience. Supporting a convict can be sketchy. Whatever the reason, while Joseph sat in prison feeling rejected, God worked a mighty plan, bigger even than Joseph's dreams.

Pharaoh had two dreams. In the first, seven skinny cattle ate seven fat cattle, but didn't gain any weight. In the second, seven wind-scorched heads of grain swallowed up seven healthy heads. These dreams troubled Pharaoh, but not one of his wisest men could tell him what they meant. Out of the shadows, the cupbearer finally comes forward. He's reminded of his promise to Joseph, and I speculate he's hoping his friend will secure his position in Pharaoh's court.

After thirteen years of slavery in a foreign land, God reveals His big plan. As Joseph stands before Pharaoh listening to the visions, God gives him the message of the dreams. Seven years of abundance will be followed by seven years of famine. Joseph advises Pharaoh to appoint a wise man to oversee Egypt and prepare the country for the years of disparity. God had not forgotten Joseph. In a matter of minutes Joseph rose from slave in prison to Egypt's second in command, and for the next seven years Joseph gathered stores so the nation would have plenty during the years of famine. God had not forgotten Joseph.

OPENING ACTIVITY   5 Minutes
  Lesson Review

BIBLE LESSON   10 Minutes
  Genesis 41

HELPING THEM REMEMBER

  MEMORY VERSE   5 Minutes
    Hebrews 13:5

  GAME   5-10 Minutes
    Memory
    Materials Needed: Any Memory Game or the cards from the back of this lesson

  CRAFT   10-20 Minutes
    Crown
    Materials Needed: Construction Paper, Pipe Cleaners, Transparent Tape and Duct Tape or Masking Tape, Scissors (not good scissors), OPTIONAL: Sticky gems

  ACTIVITY   5-10 Minutes
    Rainbow Coloring Page
    Materials Needed: Coloring Page from the end of this lesson, crayons

CLOSING MOMENTS   5 Minutes
  Clean Up and Prayer Time

The Life of Joseph Lesson Seven: God Never Leaves Us Alone

OPENING ACTIVITY   5 Minutes

Lesson Review

SAY: Guess who we're going to talk about today. *(Allow for answers)*
So what do you remember about Joseph? *(Allow for answers)*

DO: Encourage the kids to remember at least one thing from each of the first six lessons. Affirm all correct answers and try to redirect the incorrect ones.

- Joseph's father, Jacob, treated Joseph like the favorite son and gave him a beautiful coat

- Joseph had two dreams that made him believe one day his father, mother and brothers would bow to him. (When they mention the dreams, ask: "What do you think Joseph thought about his two dreams after he'd been in Egypt for 13 years?")

- Joseph's brothers sold him to Ishmaelites who took him to Egypt and sold him into slavery, but God raised him to the highest position available for a slave.

- As a slave in Potiphar's house, Mrs. Potiphar lied about him, but God raised him to the highest position in the prison.

- As a prisoner, Joseph interpreted the dreams of the baker and the cupbearer. The cupbearer promised to help him get out of prison, but the cupbearer forgot.

BIBLE LESSON   10 Minutes

Genesis 41

*Have your Bible open as you tell the story
to remind the children this Joseph is a real person from Scripture.
Retell the story in your own words or use the dialogue below*

How long do you think Joseph stayed in prison waiting for the cupbearer to tell Pharaoh about him? *(Allow for answers)* Two years after he'd told the cupbearer and the baker what the dreams meant, Joseph still sat in prison. By now he'd been in Egypt for thirteen years. That's longer than most *(or you can use all if you don't have any thirteen year olds)* of you have been alive.

Do you think you'd still be trusting God after you'd been in jail for more than ten years even though you'd done nothing wrong? *(Allow for answers.)* That would be tough! But Joseph trusted God, and believe it or not, God had not forgotten Joseph.

One night Pharaoh had a dream. He saw seven fat cows standing by the river eating the grass. Then in his dream seven ugly, scrawny cows came up out of the river. Does anyone know what those skinny cows did? *(Allow for answers)* They swallowed up the fat cows. Then Pharaoh woke up. What would you think if you had a dream like that? *(Allow for answers)*

Pharaoh went back to sleep. But soon he had another dream. He saw seven beautiful heads of grain growing from a single stalk. Does anyone know what a head of grain looks like? *(Allow for answers and show picture from the end of the lesson)* Can you guess what happened next in his dream? *(Allow for answers)* Next to those seven wonderful heads of grain, seven dried up heads of grain sprouted up. These heads of grain looked horrible, and they swallowed up the good heads of grain.

The next morning Pharaoh couldn't get the dreams off his mind. He was sure they meant something, but no one in the kingdom could help him. Pharaoh told everyone who came in the room about the dreams.

Finally the cupbearer spoke up. He said, "Today I remember a promise I made and forgot. When I made you angry two years ago, the baker and I had dreams. A Hebrew man in prison told us what our dreams meant, and everything happened just the way he said it would.

Of course Pharaoh wanted to see Joseph as soon as possible. So they cleaned him up and brought him to the king. Pharaoh told Joseph all about his dreams and asked him to explain what they meant.

Joseph said, "I cannot do it." What do you think Pharaoh thought when he heard that? *(Allow for answers)* But Joseph wasn't finished. He said, "I can't do it, but God will give you the answer you're looking for."

And Joseph went on to tell Pharaoh, "The seven fat cow and the seven good heads of grain mean that there will be seven years of abundance, all the gardens will grow well. But the skinny cows and the bad heads of grain mean that seven years of famine will follow the seven years of abundance." Who can tell me about a famine? *(Allow for answers.)* During a famine, there's no rain and nothing grows. Without corn and wheat and other crops, there's nothing to eat. Trees die, so fruit won't grow. The animals can't eat, so there's no meat.

Joseph told Pharaoh to find the wisest man to put in charge of the land. During the years of abundance, the wise man should collect grain from the people and store it so they'd have plenty during the famine. Pharaoh thought Joseph was the wisest man he'd ever met, so he put Joseph in charge. Now Joseph was second in command in all Egypt.

Even though his brothers treated him badly, Potiphar's wife lied about him, and the cupbearer forgot about him, God always had the best in mind for him. Even though it meant he had to be a slave and sit in prison for thirteen years, God had bigger plans. God never forgot Joseph, and He never forgets us.

HELPING THEM REMEMBER

MEMORY VERSE   5 Minutes
Hebrews 13:5

God said "I will never leave you or turn my back on you."
Hebrews 13:5

Repeat the verse several times, then move into the game. Use it to remind the children God watches over us and remembers us even when things aren't going our way.

GAME   5-10 Minutes
Memory
Materials Needed: Any Memory Game or the cards from the back of this lesson

PREPARE: Create and cut apart two matching sets of cards from the pages in the back or secure a memory game. If you have a small group of younger children, use only two or three pair per child. If you have a class larger than 10, be prepared to divide them into groups of 10 with one memory game for each group.

SAY: Today we're going to play a game to see if your memory is better than the cupbearer's.

DO: Shuffle or mix up the cards and lay them face down in the middle of the table and have the children gather round. They should take turns choosing only two cards. If these cards match, they may keep those cards and try again. Continue this process taking turns around the table until all of the cards are chosen. The child with the most cards wins. You may have a prize for the winner if you like. Play as many rounds as time permits.

SAY: Was it difficult to remember where the pictures were? *(Allow for answers.)* Do you always remember your promises? *(Allow for answers.)* We're humans so sometimes we forget. We need reminders like the string on your finger. But God never forgets. Sometimes it feels like He's taking a long time like He did with Joseph, and sometimes things won't go our way. But God never forgets us, He never leaves us, and He will never turn His back on us.

CRAFT   10-20 Minutes

Crown

Materials Needed: Construction Paper, Pipe Cleaners, Transparent Tape and Duct Tape or Masking Tape, Scissors (not good scissors) or wire cutters OPTIONAL: Sticky gems

1. Allow each child to pick
    - their favorite color of construction paper
    - four pipe cleaners in one color
    - three pipe cleaners in a second color

2. Cut the construction paper in half longways and tape the two halves together with transparent tape, put the paper around the child's head and mark where it will need taped together, but don't connect it yet.

3. Cut the four pipe cleaners in half (if you only have good scissors, use wire cutters for these)

4. Cut the three pipe cleaners in thirds

5. Bend the long pipe cleaners into arcs (rainbow shapes) and lay them evenly spaced from one end to the mark. Allow the arcs to stick up from the construction paper. (See sample in side column)

6. Bend the short pipe cleaners into arcs and put them in the center of the long pipe cleaners

7. Use Duct Tape or Masking tape to fasten the pipe cleaners to the construction paper.

8. OPTIONAL: Add gems or allow kids to decorate the other side as time permits

9. Join the crown's ends at the point you marked earlier and let the kids wear their crowns.

SAY: These bumps along the top of our crown can remind us of Joseph's chains. He was a prisoner for a long time, thirteen years. Are any of you thirteen yet? *(Allow for*

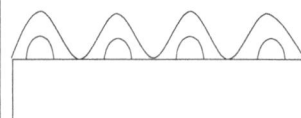

56

answers.) Joseph was a slave and a prisoner for longer than (*most of*) you have been alive. But God never forgot Joseph, and he never turned His back on Joseph. God always had a plan. The crown can remind us that Joseph went from Prisoner to Prince in just one day. God can do amazing things!

ACTIVITY   5-10 Minutes

Rainbow Coloring Page

Materials Needed: Coloring Page from the end of this lesson, crayons

Allow children to color the picture while you review the lesson. Before you finish explain why a rainbow reminds us God keeps his promises.

SAY: Thousands of years ago a flood covered the entire world, but God saved Noah and his family. After Noah came out of the ark, God showed him a rainbow and told him the rainbow would always remind Him of His promise to never forget humans and never destroy them with a flood over the whole world again. Ever since then the rainbow has been a symbol of God's promise. Every time you see a rainbow, remember God never forgets you. He will never leave you or turn his back on you.

CLOSING MOMENTS   5 Minutes

Clean Up and Prayer Time

Encourage the children to pick up pipe cleaner pieces and other remnants of their craft. Ask them to push in their chairs and gather in a circle. Then close with the prayer below or pray spontaneously.

Tremendous God,

I thank you that you never forget me. I praise you that you never forget one of these children. We are grateful that you never leave us alone. Help us to remember you always keep your promises.

In Jesus' precious Name, Amen

The Rainbow

A symbol of God's
promise to
Never Forget Us

God said,
"I will never leave
you or turn my
back on you."
Hebrews 13:5

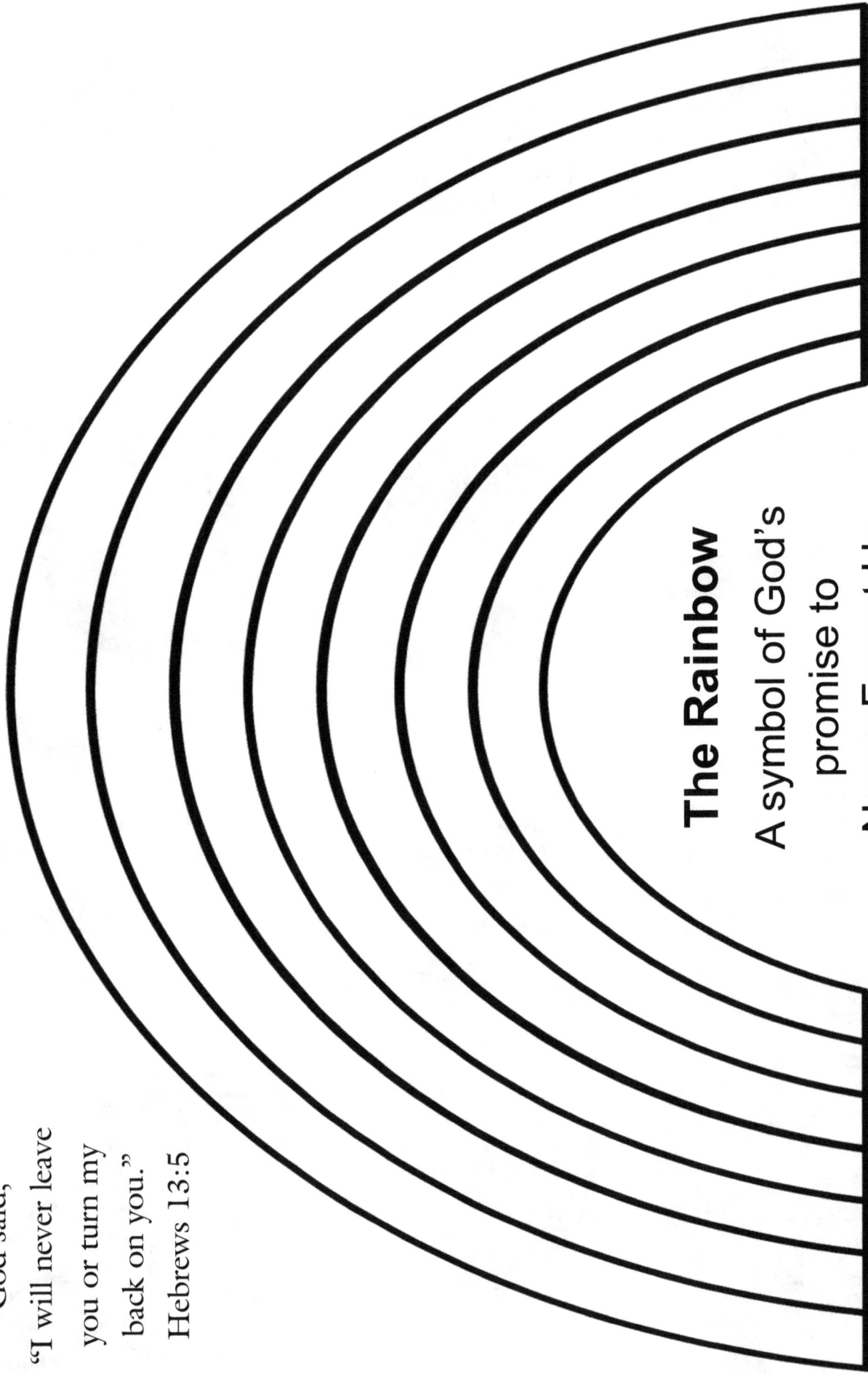

The Life of Joseph

Lesson Eight: God Has Bigger Plans

INTRODUCTION/LEADER'S DEVOTION

Overnight Joseph moved from prisoner to prince. For seven years he organized and oversaw grain collection in Egypt's capital city. At the end of that seven years everyone in the country was grateful. Four hundred miles away, Joseph's family felt the effects.

As Jacob and his other sons began to see their stores depleted, the patriarch sent the ten older boys to Egypt. When they arrived, they bowed to the 40 year-old governor of Egypt. He'd changed a good bit since they'd sold him at age 17. So although Joseph recognized his brothers immediately, they didn't realize they knew the Egyptian in charge. Joseph pretended he thought they were spies so he could question them and find out about his father and other brother. To make sure they came back, he imprisoned Simeon and demanded they return with Benjamin to prove they told the truth.

When their food ran out again, Jacob told his sons to return to Egypt. And though the old man protested, they took Benjamin. Upon their arrival, Joseph made arrangements for them to eat dinner with him. The sight of Benjamin brought him to tears, but he contained himself. How could his brothers know God had a plan when they sold him into slavery? Would they be shocked to find out Yahweh used their brother to save the world?

Joseph's story is the perfect opportunity to help children see God has plans so big we could not imagine the way He will take care of things and provide for the ones He loves.

OPENING ACTIVITY   5 Minutes
Joseph's Life in Review

BIBLE LESSON   10 Minutes
Genesis 41:53-43:34

HELPING THEM REMEMBER

MEMORY VERSE   5 Minutes
Isaiah 55:9

CRAFT   10-20 Minutes
Memory Verse Necklace
Materials Needed: String or Yarn, Tubular Pasta, Markers

GAME   5-10 Minutes
Musical Chairs with a Twist
Materials Needed: One chair for each child, Music, a coin, poker chip or token
Music suggestions: "God Provides" by Tamela Mann; "Our God" or "Good, Good Father" by Chris Tomlin

ACTIVITY   5-10 Minutes
The Story of Esther

CLOSING MOMENTS   5 Minutes
Clean Up and Prayer Time

The Life of Joseph Lesson Eight: God Has Bigger Plans

OPENING ACTIVITY   5 Minutes

Joseph's Life in Review

We've had seven lessons about Joseph. Let's see if we can remember what we've learned. *(Encourage the children to tell you what happened to Joseph as well as what we learned about God)*

What Happened to Joseph	**What we Learned about God**
1. Joseph was Jacob's favorite. Jacob gave him a beautiful coat.	1. We're God's favorite.
2. Joseph had two dreams that made it seem he'd be in charge of his mother, father and brothers someday, and then he bragged about them.	2. We have to stay humble even though we know we're God's favorite.
3. Joseph's brothers were jealous so they sold him into slavery.	3. God tells us to love our enemies, even the bullies.
4. Joseph became Potiphar's slave. But while a slave, he did what honored God even when it was hard, and God blessed him.	4. Always follow God and do the right thing and God will bless us.
5. Potiphar's wife lied about Joseph, so Joseph ended up in prison.	5. Lies hurt. Don't lie about others.
6. The baker and the cupbearer had dreams, but they forgot about Joseph.	6. Always remember to keep your promises.
7. Pharaoh had a dream and the cupbearer finally remembered Joseph sitting in prison, so Joseph becomes second in command in Egypt.	7. Even though people forget us and forget their promises, God never forgets.

How many of you thought we'd heard all of Joseph's story? *(Allow for answers.)* Last week we had a pretty happy ending didn't we? But what if I told you there's more?!

BIBLE LESSON   10 Minutes

Genesis 41:53-43:15

Read Genesis 41:53-43:15 as you prepare.
Have your Bible open as you tell the story to remind the children this Joseph is a real person from Scripture. Retell the story in your own words or use the dialogue below

For the next seven years Joseph gathered grain from every person in Egypt. He created big barns and silos to store all the extra food. After seven years, the famine began just as Joseph said. Who can tell me what a famine is? *(Allow for answers.)* For seven years there was little or no rain. And what happens when there's no rain? *(Allow for answers.)* And what happens when nothing grows? *(Allow for answers.)* Eventually even the animals didn't have anything to eat, so there was no grain, no fruit, no

*See Genesis 46:26-27

66 descendants
+ 10 wives
+ Jacob

vegetables and no meat.

Even though Joseph lived a long way from Jacob and his brothers, the famine affected them too. It was more than four hundred miles, but the rain didn't fall on Jacob either. Jacob's eleven other sons still lived nearby. All were married and all had children. The Bible tells us they needed to feed more than 70 people.*

But they hadn't stored grain like Joseph. So Jacob and his family began to run out of food. Even without television or the internet, word reached Jacob Egypt had supplies. So he had no choice but to send his sons on the long trip. Ten boys left Canaan to go to Egypt, only Benjamin stayed behind.

Twenty-five years had passed since Joseph's brothers had sold him to the Ishmaelites. Joseph had never been allowed to send a letter, so his brothers thought he was a slave somewhere or had been killed. They didn't even know for sure where he'd been taken, and they had no idea Joseph had become second in command in Egypt.

When the brothers arrived in Egypt, they went straight to the grain storehouses to buy food for the family. The overseer of the grain was there. Who was the overseer? *(Allow for answers.)* Yes, Joseph. Because he had this important Egyptian position, Joseph wore Egyptian clothes and kept his beard shaved because Egyptians never grew beards. Joseph walked and talked like an Egyptian.

When he saw his brothers, he immediately knew them. However, because Joseph now looked like a grown man and acted like an Egyptian, his brothers didn't recognize him. So when he walked over to talk to them, all of the brothers bowed down in front of him since he was like the king. What do you think Joseph remembered when the brothers were on their knees in front of them? *(Allow for answers.)* Joseph's dreams from long ago came true. He dreamt the moon and the stars and his brothers' bundles of grain would bow before him, and it happened right in front of him.

Since they didn't recognize him, Joseph questioned them about their family, but he pretended he didn't know their language. He used an interpreter and found out his father and Benjamin were alive and well. But he didn't tell his brothers he was too.

Instead he accused the brothers of being spies. He put them in prison for three days. When he let them out, he kept one brother in prison. He told them he wanted proof they weren't lying. To get their brother Simeon out of prison, they had to come back with their younger brother to prove they were telling the truth.

Joseph's nine brothers returned home. Time passed, and they ran out of food again, but this time they had to take Benjamin. Jacob didn't want Benjamin to go with them, but they knew without their youngest brother the overseer wouldn't give them any food and Simeon would stay in prison. In fact, they were afraid they all might end up in prison.

Jacob finally allowed Benjamin to go to Egypt. So they travelled to get more food for the family, and when they arrived, they introduced Benjamin to the second most powerful man in Egypt. But Joseph still didn't reveal his true identity.

MEMORY VERSE   5 Minutes

Isaiah 55:9

Just as the heavens are higher than the earth,
so are my ways higher than your ways
and my thoughts higher than your thoughts.
Isaiah 55:9

SAY: For seventeen years Joseph had a horrible life. He was a slave and in prison. Would you like to live like that? *(Allow for answers.)* And even though God had given him those dreams to tell him someday everyone would bow down to him, I think it would have been hard to live in Egypt as a slave with no family around.

What would have happened to Jacob and his family if Joseph hadn't been taken to Egypt to help Pharaoh? *(Allow for answers.)* If no one had interpreted Pharaoh's dreams, no grain would have been stored. Everyone would have starved. Seven years is too long to go without food. Jacob, Joseph and all the brothers would have died.

God makes plans bigger than we can imagine. Today's memory verse reminds us of this.

DO: Say today's Bible verse a few times stopping at the end of each line for children to repeat. Be sure to include the reference (Isaiah 55:9) as a fourth line.

CRAFT   10-20 Minutes

Memory Verse Necklace

Materials Needed: String or Yarn, Tubular Pasta, Markers

PREPARE: If you have a large number of Kindergarten and Pre-Kindergarten, prepare the pasta before class. Using eight piece of Penne, Ziti or Rigatoni, write "God's Ways Are Higher Than My Ways" Isaiah 55:9 with one word on each piece - If you use Penne, you could write the words so the slanted ends alternate and fall together nicely. Also write the phrase and reference on a white board or a large piece of construction paper for the older kids to copy from.

DO: Pass out a 30"-36" string and ten pieces of pasta to each student, giving the younger ones the pre-written pasta. Allow older students to use the markers to write the verse and reference on eight pieces. Encourage all students to decorate the final two as they wish.

String the pasta with one decorated piece on each end, ensuring the words read right to left. Have the children lay out the string and verify the words are in the right order before you tie. Tie the string so it will fit over the head.

SAY: Does anyone know what these pasta noodles are made from? *(Allow for answers.)* Noodles are made from flour and eggs, and millers use grain to make flour. Why would we use grain to make our craft today? *(Allow for answers.)*

Our noodles should remind us God sent Joseph ahead of his family to store up grain. What if Joseph hadn't been sent to Egypt by his brothers? *(Allow for answers.)* If Joseph hadn't been in Egypt, no one would have told Pharaoh his dream and no grain would have been saved for those seven years. God had plans bigger than anyone could imagine. So our pasta necklaces with our memory verse can remind us of Joseph and God's big plan.

GAME   10 Minutes

Musical Chairs with a Twist

Materials Needed: One chair for each child, music, a coin, poker chip or token

Music suggestions: "God Provides" by Tamela Mann; "Our God" or "Good, Good Father" by Chris Tomlin

DO: As in a traditional game of Musical Chairs, put chairs in a circle with backs together. Use one less chair than the number of children you have. As you play the music the children will walk around the chairs. When the music stops, each will scramble for a seat, the one left standing is out.

TWIST: Secretly give the token to one of the children. You might have all children stand in a line with eyes closed and hands out. Stop at each child and close their hand, but one child will have the token when you're done. This token will allow them to stay in the game if they don't get a seat. They will forfeit the token when they need to stay in the game, and you'll use the same method to give the token to another child.

SAY: Today we're going to play music chairs. *(If you have children who don't know the game, explain.)* This token *(show the piece)* will make the game a bit different. If you have this token, you can give it to me to stay in the game if you don't get a chair. No one can know you have the token. *(Optional: If someone figures out who has the token, you take the token and secretly give it to another)*

DO: Play the game for as long as you have time. You may optionally have a prize for the winner.

SAY: Just like you never knew who I might give the token too, we don't know who God might choose to do a big job like Joseph. Joseph's brothers thought he was arrogant. Because they were jealous of him, they sold him to a caravan passing by. But God had a plan they knew nothing about. God chose Joseph to rescue the whole world from a famine. Even Joseph didn't know God's plan for twenty-five years. You never know when God might pick you. He might have big plans.

When you held your hand out, you were ready for me to put the token in it. In the same way we need to be ready for God to use us in His plans.

ACTIVITY   5-10 Minutes

The Story of Esther

Share this story with the children

The Bible tells the story of another person about the same age as Joseph who was taken from her family. This girl's name was Hadassah. Can you say Hadassah? *(Encourage kids to repeat.)* Hadassah lived with her cousin Mordecai. That's another strange name, can you say Mordecai? *(Encourage kids to repeat)* Mordecai and Hadassah were Jews living far from Israel.

One day the king's men saw Hadassah and noticed her beauty, so they took her to the King's house because he was looking for a new beautiful wife. In the king's house, they called her by her other name, Esther. After a year, the King married Esther, so she became the queen. But no one in the castle knew she was a Jew.

Years went by and Esther enjoyed being a queen. But the king had a friend who hated Jews. He hated them so much he wanted them all killed. So he asked the king to kill them. What do you think the king said? *(Allow for answers.)* It's hard to believe, but the king agreed! He issued a decree that all the Jews in his kingdom would die on a certain day.

When Mordecai heard the news, he snuck over to see Queen Esther. He knew the only way the Jews could be saved would be with Esther's help. But Esther was afraid of the king. The king hadn't talked to her for a while, and she wasn't allowed to just go in and talk to him. .

Esther put her fear aside and decided to help save her people. She invited the king and his friend to a great feast two days in a row. After dinner on the second day she told him his friend wanted to kill her and her family. The king was furious! He sent his friend away to die and saved all the Jewish people.

What would've happened if Hadassah/Esther hadn't been taken away to the king's palace? *(Allow for answers.)* Being taken away from her family was difficult. There's no way Esther could have known God planned to use her to save thousands of people. God's plans were bigger than Esther and Joseph could imagine, and He has plans for you too!

CLOSING MOMENTS   5 Minutes

Clean Up and Prayer Time

Encourage the children to pick up loose pasta and other remnants of their craft. Ask them to push in their chairs and gather in a circle. Then close with the prayer below or pray spontaneously.

Almighty God,

Thank you for your big plans. We praise you that you have ways and thoughts we can't imagine. When we go through difficult times like Joseph, help us to remember you have big plans. Remind us that you can use even our hardest times if we trust you and honor you.

In Jesus' precious Name, Amen

The Life of Joseph

Lesson Nine: Bitter or Better?

INTRODUCTION/LEADER'S DEVOTION

Jacob had put off the second trip to Egypt as long as possible because the man in charge insisted the brothers bring his beloved Benjamin, but the food buy went off without a hitch. They recovered Simeon bought their grain and headed home completely unaware that Joseph's servants had returned all their gold and hidden a chalice in Benjamin's saddle bags. One might think Joseph vengeful for sending soldiers to arrest his brothers for stealing a chalice he had planted. But as the story unfolds we realize Egypt's second in command had no desire for revenge.

Imagine for a moment what it must have been like to have been Joseph's brothers the day he revealed himself. Drug into the capital by soldiers, they stood before Egypt's leader pleading for Benjamin's life. When the ruler lost it, the eleven men stood there more confused than ever. And when he finally composed himself enough for the reintroduction, I picture Benjamin beaming with joy while they others relived scenes of a young Joseph crying out from a pit and begging not to be sold. What would the second strongest man in the known world do to them?

Joseph's imprisonment gave him a lot of time to become bitter, instead he used them to bring glory to God. His reward was nine years living out God's purpose. Recognizing how God used his brother's evil plan for good shaped him into a better man. Joseph didn't seek revenge on his brothers because he knew God had used their evil for good.

OPENING ACTIVITY	5 Minutes
Do You Want Revenge?	
BIBLE LESSON	10 Minutes
Genesis 44:1-34 & 45:1-28	
HELPING THEM REMEMBER	
MEMORY VERSE	5 Minutes
Genesis 50:20	
GAME	5-10 Minutes
Charades	
Materials Needed: Slips of paper from last page of this lesson	
CRAFT	10-20 Minutes
Mask	
Materials Needed: Paper plates or construction paper, scissors, markers or crayons, string	
ACTIVITY	5-10 Minutes
What would Joseph Do?	
Materials Needed: Opening Questions	
CLOSING MOMENTS	5 Minutes
Clean Up and Prayer Time	

The Life of Joseph Lesson Nine: Bitter or Better?

OPENING ACTIVITY   5 Minutes

Do You Want Revenge?

Use the following questions to help kids understand how easy it is to seek revenge. Resist the urge to praise answers that promote peace. We'll revisit these later. This activity is information gathering. Each child will probably have at least one scenario that stirs a need to get even.

1. If someone hits you, what do you want to do? *(If no one says, "hit back," ask if anyone would try to do that.)*

2. When someone steals your things, what do you want to do? *(If no one says, "get them in trouble," ask if anyone would try to do that.)*

3. When someone lies about you and gets you in trouble, what do you want to do? *(If no one says, "Lie about them or try to get them in trouble," ask if anyone would try to do that.)*

4. If someone is mean to your friend or your sister or brother, what do you want to do?

5. If someone takes credit for your work, what do you want to do?

6. If you were Joseph, and your brothers had put you in a deep hole and then sold you as a slave what would you want to do when you saw them?

BIBLE LESSON   10 Minutes

Genesis 44:1-34 & 45:1-28

Read Genesis 44 & 45 as you prepare.
Have your Bible open as you tell the story
to remind the children this Joseph is a real person from Scripture.
Retell the story in your own words or use the dialogue below

Joseph had every right to want revenge. Do you know what revenge is? *(Allow for answers.)* Sometimes when people do bad things we want them to pay for their crime. When we hit someone who hits us, that's revenge. So what do you think Joseph wanted to do to his brothers? *(Allow for answers)* Well, let's continue with Joseph's story.

Joseph had been a slave and a prisoner in Egypt for thirteen years before Pharaoh made him governor. He's spent nine years in charge of all the food. How long had it been since Joseph's brothers had seen him? *(Allow for answers)* Joseph had been in Egypt for 22 years. So he looked very different than when his brothers sold him to the Ishmaelites. They had no idea those traders would sell him in Egypt, and I'm sure they never thought he'd end up a ruler.

When Joseph's brothers came back for food the second time, they brought Benjamin just like he asked. But Joseph decided to play a trick on his brothers. He asked his servants to put all his brothers' money back in their bags and hide his special cup in Benjamin's bags. Then he sent them on their way.

The brothers hadn't traveled far when Joseph sent men to retrieve his special cup. The soldiers arrested Benjamin when they found it in his bags, but all the brothers returned to Egypt because they couldn't go home without Jacob's new favorite son.

The brothers told Joseph they didn't know how the cup got in Benjamin's bag, and they told him their father would die if they didn't bring Benjamin home. Even face to face with Joseph, the brothers still didn't recognize him. Joseph couldn't take it any longer. He sent all the Egyptians out and started crying. He cried so hard he could hardly talk, but he finally let his brothers know who he was.

His brothers were speechless. They thought Joseph was a slave somewhere or dead. They didn't expect to find him as the ruler of Egypt. They expected Joseph to be angry and bitter, but Joseph told them not to worry. He explained about the famine, and said he believed God brought him to Egypt for just this moment. Joseph hugged and kissed his brothers. Then he sent them home to get Jacob. The whole family moved to Egypt to be with Joseph during the famine.

Joseph could have been angry with his brothers. He had every right to plot revenge and get even, but instead of being bitter, Joseph spent all his years in Egypt becoming better. He forgave his brothers and loved them.

HELPING THEM REMEMBER

MEMORY VERSE   5 Minutes

Genesis 50:20

> [20] *You intended to harm me, but God intended it for good*
> *to accomplish what is now being done, the saving of many lives.*
> *Genesis 50:20*

DO: Repeat this verse with the children several times. If you have a young group, use just the first line.

SAY: Our memory verse today is what Joseph told his brothers when their father died. For 17 years Joseph's brothers worried about what Joseph would do to get revenge, but Joseph forgave them.

DO: Repeat the verse a few more times.

SAY: Bad things happen to everyone, but if we remember God uses everything for good, like Joseph did we can become better instead of bitter.

GAME   5-10 Minutes

Charades

Materials Needed: The last page of this lesson cut into strips with all the strips in a bowl

DO: Choose one of the older children to begin. Have the student take one slip of paper from the bowl and act it out. Decide before you begin whether you will allow sound effects. The child who guesses the charade may perform the next one. Play continues as long as you have time. When any child gets a second turn, choose one of the kids who has a difficult time guessing to take their turn at the charade.

SAY: We pretended to be something else to have fun. Did you have a good time guessing each charade? *(Allow for answers.)* Did any of you think <name a child> was really a <name the charade they performed>? *(Allow for answers.)* Joseph played a charade with his brothers. He pretended to be Egyptian, but Joseph did his charade so well his brothers didn't recognize him. When Joseph finally revealed himself, his brothers were afraid, but was Joseph angry? *(Allow for answers)* No, because Joseph knew God had everything planned for a bigger purpose. So Joseph never became bitter; He became better.

CRAFT　　　　　　　　　　　　　　　　　　　　　　10-20 Minutes

Mask

Materials Needed: Paper plates or construction paper, scissors, markers or crayons, string

SAY: Today we're going to make masks to remind us Joseph's brothers didn't recognize him when they arrived in Egypt.

DO: Give each student a paper plate or a piece of construction paper. If you use construction paper, allow the kids to draw a shape for their mask and cut it out. Next help the students cut eye holes.

Punch holes in the sides and tie strings through the holes.

Allow students to decorate their masks any way they like, then put the masks on so they can see what they look like. Provide a mirror if available.

SAY: Do you recognize everyone? *(Allow for answers.)* Is there anyone here you might not know if you didn't know how they made their mask? *(Allow for answers.)* What if they were grown up with this mask on? *(Allow for answers.)* Joseph had grown up a lot when his brothers saw him in Egypt. They didn't recognize him. Plus they expected him to be mad at them, but how did Joseph feel when he saw his brothers? *(Allow for answers.)* Joseph was very happy to see them. He'd forgiven them long before they got to Egypt. Joseph was the second most powerful person in Egypt. He could have put them in jail and never told them he was their brother. But Joseph chose to be a better person, not a bitter person.

ACTIVITY　　　　　　　　　　　　　　　　　　　　　5-10 Minutes

What would Joseph Do?

Materials Needed: Opening Questions

SAY: So, now that we know Joseph better, let's look at those first questions we asked today and see if we can decide what Joseph would do. *(In every instance help the children understand Joseph probably would not have retaliated.)*

1. If someone hit Joseph, what do you think he would do?

2. If someone stole Joseph's things, what do you think he would do?

3. If someone lied about Joseph, what do you think he would do? *(If you have time talk a minute about Potiphar's wife. Now that Joseph was powerful, he could have had her put in prison for lying, but he didn't)*

4. If someone had been mean to Joseph's friend or his sister or brothers, what do you think he would do?

5. If someone took credit for Joseph's work, what do you think he would do?

6. Joseph's brothers put him in a deep hole and then sold him as a slave. What did Joseph do when he saw them?

SAY: Do you remember how much power Joseph had? If Joseph had spent those thirteen years being angry at his brothers, he might have punished them for being so mean, but Joseph knew that wasn't what God would want him to do. Joseph spent those thirteen years getting to know God better so He was able to show love and forgiveness to his brothers.

Notes, Scribbles, Jots & Doodles

Clean Up and Prayer Time

Encourage the children to pick up scraps of paper and other remnants of their craft. Ask them to push in their chairs and gather in a circle. Then close with the prayer below or pray spontaneously.

Forgiving God,

Thank you that you always forgive us. We praise you for Joseph. Thank you for letting him show us how to become better instead of bitter. Help us to always get closer to you when people are mean to us, and help us to forgive them.

In Jesus' precious Name, Amen

Charade Suggestions
(add your own ideas or remove the ones your group will have a hard time with)

Bear	Snake	Someone eating spaghetti
Lion	Bird	Weight Lifter
Someone who stepped on Legos	Dog	Cat
Racecar Driver	Mom cooking dinner	Dad shaving
Someone on a cell phone	Tree	Elephant
Astronaut	Robot	Hula Dancer
Ballerina	Trumpet Player	Rock Star
Photographer	Monkey	Train
Fish	Painter	Scarecrow

The Life of Joseph

Lesson Ten: God Uses Joseph to Provide for His People

INTRODUCTION/LEADER'S DEVOTION

Pharaoh sent wagons to Canaan to bring Jacob and his family back to Egypt. Seventy people made the long journey. Pharaoh gave them land just outside the capital city where they could graze their many flocks and herds. Five more years of famine threatened the entire region. Everyone in Egypt became dependent on the Pharaohs, first bringing all their money to buy food, then their livestock and finally they sold their land and their bodies. Some believe that Egypt's government owning all the land still in the early 21st Century was the result of this seven year famine.

The Bible says that Egypt and Canaan wasted away because of the famine. Without Joseph in place collecting the grain and then distributing it, both nations may have been wiped out, and Israel along with them. But God used Joseph to provide for His people.

Most of the time, we'd prefer God provide with miracles and grand gestures, but often the Almighty uses people to carry out His plan. We need to be on the lookout for times when God wants to use us to provide for the hungry and take care of the poor. It's good for the children to understand sometimes God provides through us.

OPENING ACTIVITY   5 Minutes
  Kids in Need
  Materials Needed: Photos of kids in poverty, ask you congregation for photos of kids they sponsor or check out the World Vision site

BIBLE LESSON   10 Minutes
  Genesis 45:16 - 47:30

HELPING THEM REMEMBER

  MEMORY VERSE   5 Minutes
    Psalm 111:5

  GAME   5-10 Minutes
    Rice Race
    Materials Needed: Two pounds of rice for every sixteen children, four big bowls for every sixteen children, plastic spoons

  CRAFT   10-20 Minutes
    Grain Collage
    Materials Needed: Rice, dried corn, oatmeal, wheat kernels

  ACTIVITY   5-10 Minutes
    How God Provides
    Materials Needed: Photos from Opening

CLOSING MOMENTS   5 Minutes
  Clean Up and Prayer Time

The Life of Joseph Lesson Ten:
God Uses Joseph to Provide for His People

OPENING ACTIVITY   5 Minutes

Kids in Need

Materials Needed: Photos of kids in poverty, ask your congregation for photos of kids they sponsor or check out the World Vision or other social justice site

DO: Gather the photos and show one to the children.

SAY: Did you have something to eat today? What if I told you this child may not have anything to eat today? What about yesterday? *(Show a second picture)* What if I told you this child may have gotten her last meal from the garbage? *(Show all the pictures)* Each of these kids live in places where it's hard to get food. They don't have grocery stores nearby, and in some of the places food won't grow because there's no rain. Do you remember what we call it when food doesn't grow because it doesn't rain? *(Allow for answers.)* It's called famine. And who have we been talking about that lived through a famine? *(Allow for answers)* So, let's hear about the next thing Joseph did.

BIBLE LESSON   10 Minutes

Genesis 45:16 - 47:30

Read Genesis 45-47 as you prepare.
Have your Bible open as you tell the story
to remind the children this Joseph is a real person from Scripture.
Retell the story in your own words or use the dialogue below

All of the food in the world was stored in Egypt. Do you remember where the food came from? *(Allow for answers)* For seven years Joseph had been in charge. He'd collected food from all over Egypt so there'd be plenty during the seven years of famine.

After Joseph told his brother's who he was, Pharaoh sent wagons so Jacob and the rest of the family could come to Egypt. This way they'd have plenty to eat during the years of famine. Jacob was overjoyed when he discovered Joseph was still alive. He could hardly believe Joseph had risen to second in command in Egypt.

The night they left, God spoke to Jacob while he was sleeping. God said, "Don't be afraid of Egypt. Someday I'll bring all of your family back here to the Promised Land." Joseph's father, brothers, sister, and all of their families traveled to Egypt. Jacob started with 12 sons, but seventy people went with him to Egypt.

When Jacob saw Joseph, he was so happy! It had been more than 20 years since Joseph had disappeared.

Pharaoh gave Jacob and his family a large piece of land outside of the capital. They had lots of room for all their sheep. And from that day on Joseph provided his father and all his brothers and sisters all the food they needed.

Because God allowed Joseph to go to Egypt, there was food for everyone including Joseph's family. God used Joseph to provide for his family and all of Egypt when there was no food.

HELPING THEM REMEMBER

MEMORY VERSE   5 Minutes

Psalm 111:5

> *God gives food to those who trust him; he never forgets his promises.*
> *Psalm 111:5*

DO: Repeat the verse with the children a few times, pausing at the semicolon to give them time to repeat

SAY: What does it mean to trust God? *(Allow for answers)* Trusting God means counting on Him. It means believing He will do what He says.

What does this Psalm say happens to people who trust God? *(Allow for answers)* God gives food to those who trust Him. Just like He did for Jacob and the rest of Joseph's family. God provides for those who trust Him.

GAME   5-10 Minutes

Rice Race

Materials Needed: Two pounds of rice for every sixteen children, four big bowls for every sixteen children, plastic spoons

DO: Place the bowls on tables about 8 feet apart, 1/2 of the bowls on each table.

Put one bag of rice in each of the bowls on one table

Divide the children into teams of eight or less. Give each child a plastic spoon.

Decide whether the activity will be timed with the one whose moved the most rice winning, or the game will go until one team has emptied their bowl.

SAY: Just like Joseph filled the barns with grain so all the people could eat during the famine, we're going to fill bowls with grain. Each team will stand in a line. The first person in each line will put the spoon in their mouth, go to the bowl with rice, dip out a spoonful of rice without using hands and walk to their teams other bowl and put it in.

DO: Let the children finish the game. If you have a younger group, you may want to change the rules to carrying the spoon in their hand. When the game is over, talk about the grain.

SAY: Today we moved rice. This game can remind us of how Joseph collected grain for seven years then fed many families and helped save them from the famine. God put Joseph in the perfect place so God's chosen people could be saved from the famine. God provided for His people

CRAFT   10-20 Minutes

Grain Collage

Materials Needed: Rice, dried corn, oatmeal, wheat kernels or other grains, glue and copies of the bread on cardstock

1.   Give each child a copy of the bread on cardstock, glue and grain.

2. Older children might want to put darker grain in the darker section and lighter grain in the lighter sections.

3. As the kids fill in the bread with the grain tell them:

SAY: All of this grain can remind us about Joseph and the way he followed God's instructions to store grain for seven years.

What happened because God warned Joseph about the famine? *(Allow for answers.)* Because God warned Joseph and he listened, he saved grain for seven years keeping Jacob's family and all of Egypt alive during the famine.

So every time you look at this picture, I hope you think of Joseph and remember God provides for His people.

ACTIVITY   5-10 Minutes

How God Provides

Materials Needed: Photos from Opening

DO: Show the children the pictures from the opening

SAY: Each of these kids might have starved and died, but someone went into their town and showed their families how to grow food. Other people donated money so these kids could have what they needed. *(If you sponsor a child, or someone in your church sponsors a child, you might have them talk about what they do to support the child)* God uses us to help those who have less. Because people give time and money and missionaries give up their homes to live with them, these kids have enough food. God provides through His people.

CLOSING MOMENTS   5 Minutes

Clean Up and Prayer Time

Encourage the children to pick up scraps of paper and pieces of grain. Ask them to push in their chairs and gather in a circle. Then close with the prayer below or pray spontaneously.

Dear God who Provides,

Thank you that you always giving us what we need. We praise you for Joseph. Thank you for using him to provide for Jacob and his family. Help us to learn a lesson from Joseph and always listen for God when he asks us to help provide.

In Jesus' precious Name, Amen

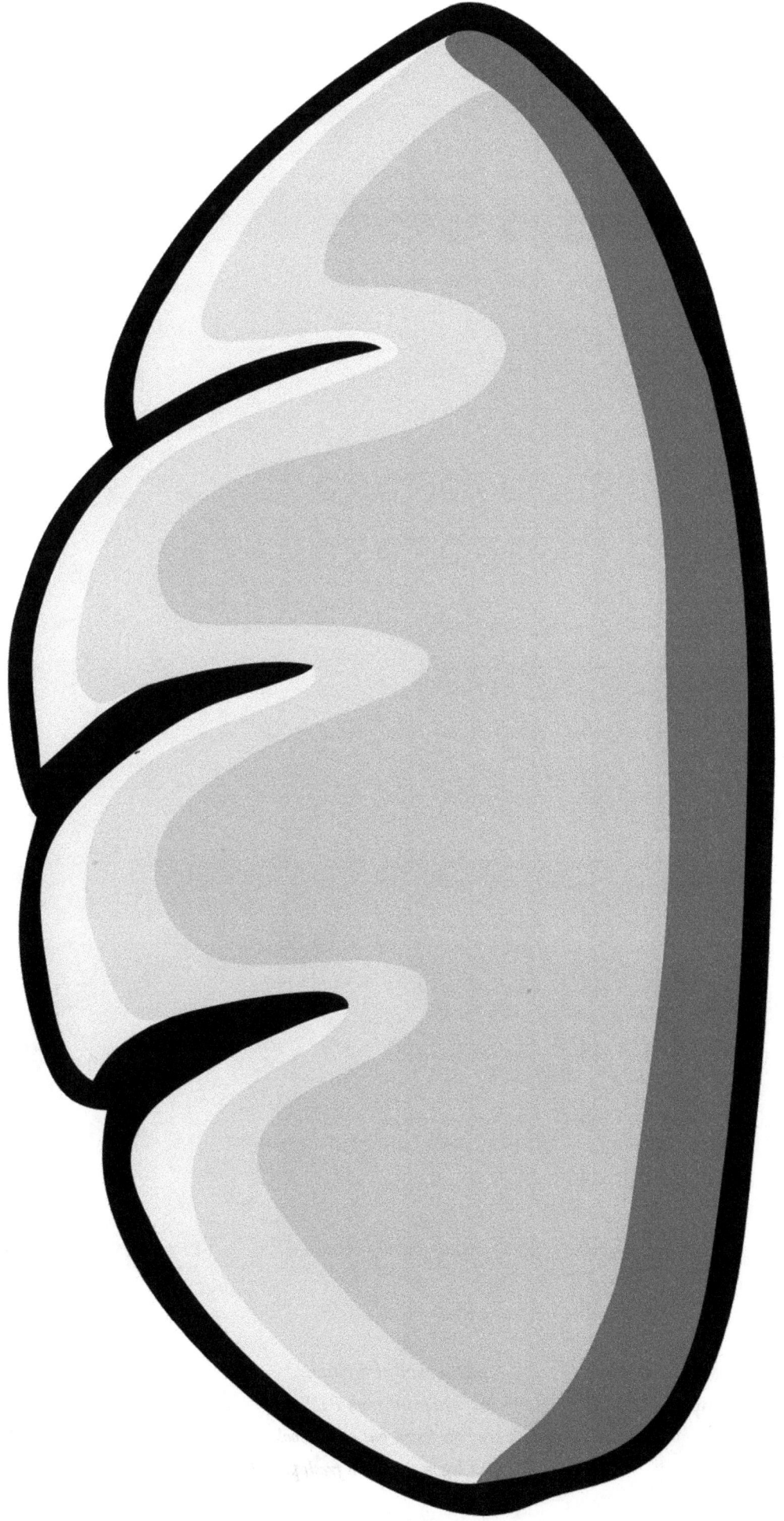

God gives food to those who trust him;
he never forgets his promises.
Psalm 111:5

Intentionally left blank
so if you print from PDF
or tear the lesson out of the book
the next lesson falls on a fresh page

The Life of Joseph

Lesson Eleven: Speaking Words of Blessing

INTRODUCTION/LEADER'S DEVOTION

In ancient times fathers spoke words of blessing over their sons before they died. The last chapters of Genesis show us Jacob's final words. While Jacob's blessing was more like prophecy, we're going to focus on the blessing.

Children as well as adults need words of blessing spoken over them often. We need to remember that all of our speech can become blessings or curses. And while we don't really believe in curses like they did a few hundred years ago, often our negativity becomes self-fulfilling prophecy. So learning to speak blessings and teaching these children to speak blessings is imperative.

OPENING ACTIVITY   15 Minutes

Speaking Words of Blessings
Materials Needed: Index Cards filled out before your ministry time

BIBLE LESSON   10 Minutes

Genesis 48-50

HELPING THEM REMEMBER

CRAFT   10-20 Minutes

Blessing Blooms
Materials Needed: 1 of each per student: Small poster board or tag board, 16 oz. water or pop bottles (must have a bumped bottom - flat bottom bottles won't work) - for the group: markers, craft paint, paper plates *(This craft will need drying time)*

MEMORY VERSE   5 Minutes

Numbers 6:24-26
Let's Learn a Bible Blessing

GAME   5-10 Minutes

Blessing Hopscotch
Materials Needed: Masking Tape and Memory Verse print out from last pages

ACTIVITY   5-10 Minutes

Singing Words of Blessing
Materials Needed: Screen to project Kari Jobe & Cody Carnes "The Blessing" or just the recording. Here's the YouTube Link: https://www.youtube.com/watch?v=uZ55mDL7dA0

CLOSING MOMENTS   5 Minutes

Clean Up and Prayer Time

The Life of Joseph Lesson Eleven
Speaking Words of Blessing

OPENING ACTIVITY   15 Minutes

Speaking Words of Blessings

Materials Needed: Index Cards filled out before your ministry time

Take some time this week to put each of your students' names on an index card. Then, under their name write one phrase of blessing. "May the Lord . . ." Each child's could be different. Here are some ideas:

. . . Watch over you and keep you safe

. . . Help you develop your _____ (name a talent your student demonstrates)

. . . Help you in school

. . . Show you how special you are

. . . Bless your family

Under the blessing write: "And Your friends think you are . . ."

During this opening activity collect blessings from the rest of the class. Using the cards you created, fill in the bottom of the card with at least three other students' blessings.

SAY: What is your favorite thing about _____?

DO: Write these things on the card. If you only have enough time to put the first three things you hear on each card that's fine. You could do more at the end if you have time. Before you finish tell each child what you wrote on their card.

BIBLE LESSON   10 Minutes

Genesis 48-50

Read Genesis 48-50 as you prepare.
Have your Bible open as you tell the story
to remind the children this Joseph is a real person from Scripture.
Retell the story in your own words or use the dialogue below

Where did we leave Joseph and his family the last time we talked about him? *(Allow for answers).* Joseph had been taken to Egypt when he was seventeen, and the rest of his family came to Egypt more than 20 years later. A lot of time had passed, and the famine was over, but Jacob and his family stayed in the land of Egypt.

During the time Jacob and Joseph lived, fathers spoke words of blessing over their sons, much like the words I wrote on your cards. They carried these blessings with them for their whole lives and worked hard to live up to them.

When Jacob was very old, he called Joseph into his house and asked him to bring his sons, Manasseh and Ephraim. Can you say Manasseh and Ephraim? *(Have the children repeat these names.)* Because Joseph had been his favorite and he missed out on more than 20 years of Joseph's life, Jacob gave an extra blessing to Joseph's two sons. Usually they didn't give their grandchildren blessings, but Jacob blessed Manasseh and Ephraim.

When Jacob blessed Joseph's sons he said, "May these boys be called by my name, and may they increase greatly."

Then, just before he died, Jacob called in all of his sons. Some of his sons received long blessings and others short. Some of them who had done very bad things in their life didn't get blessings at all; they got words of warning.

Jacob's blessing for Judah was the longest. In it Jacob said that kings would come from Judah's children, and eventually the King who would be king forever would be a descendant of Judah. Do you know who that was? *(Allow for answers.)* Jesus came from the tribe of Judah, and he is a king forever.

Gad, Asher and Naphtali each only had a one line blessing. Jacob said that Gad would be attacked, and Asher would grow wonderful food. Joseph received a long blessing, too. Jacob said that God would bless Joseph, and that all of Jacob's blessings would fall on Joseph.

After he was done blessing all of his sons, Jacob told them where he should be buried, and then he curled up in his bed, and that night he died. Do you remember how old he was? *(Allow for answers.)* Jacob was 147 years old.

What if I told you, you can bless others just like Jacob blessed his sons and I blessed you!?

HELPING THEM REMEMBER

CRAFT   10-20 Minutes

Blessing Blooms

Materials Needed: 1 of each per student: Small poster board or tag board, 16 oz. water or pop bottles (must have a bumped bottom - flat bottom bottles won't work) - for the group: markers, craft paint, paper plates *(This craft will need drying time)*

1. Give each student a piece of poster/tag board and a water/pop bottle (If you don't have enough bottles for each student, make sure there's one for each paint color and have half the students draw their pot on the bottom while the other half makes their blooms)

2. Put a puddle of paint on each plate (a different color on each plate)

3. Have children choose one color then dip the bottom of the bottle into the paint and press the bottle onto their paper. Three or four blooms across the top of the page should be enough.

4. Allow each one to draw a pot on the bottom of the page.

5. You may want to let the paint dry a bit before putting the stems on. If so, move to the "SAY" portion and then the Memory Verse. After you've completed other activities, draw a squiggly stem from the base of each flower to the pot using markers. Add leaves to your stems, too, if desired.

SAY: Flowers are a blessing from God. They brighten up a room and cheer up people who are sad and sick. Each time you see a flower, think of one blessing God has given you for every bloom you see. Can you think of a blessing for each flower on your picture? *(Allow for answers)*

"The LORD bless you ** and keep you;
The LORD make His face ** shine upon you,
And be gracious to you;
The Lord turn his ** face toward you,
and give you peace."
Numbers 6:24-26

Have the children repeat the verse a few times pausing at the breaks. **
then move into the game.

GAME   5-10 Minutes

Blessing Hopscotch

Materials Needed: Masking Tape and Memory Verse written on 8 pages (feel free to use more if you like) OPTIONAL: Timer

DO: Place tape on the floor like this: (You could also use sidewalk chalk if you are outside or have a cement floor that's easily cleaned) Place the paper for the verses in the squares as shown

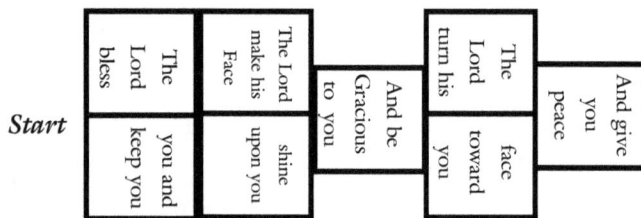

Start

The Lord bless / The you and keep you	The Lord make his Face / shine upon you	The Lord Gracious to you / And be	The Lord turn his / The face toward you	And give you peace

SAY: Today we're going to play blessing hopscotch. You may hop on the squares after you say that part of the verse. (*If you plan to time the children, tell them the one who can do it the fastest will win*)

DO: If you have time for a second round, take three pieces of paper off (the three on the right of the two squared rows), and have children go again. If you have time for a third round, you could remove two more or all of the papers.

SAY: This blessing is as old as the Bible. You can speak this blessing over your friends and family asking God to bless them and protect them.

ACTIVITY   5 Minutes

Singing Words of Blessing

Materials Needed: Screen to project Kari Jobe & Cody Carnes "The Blessing" or just the recording. Here's the YouTube Link: https://www.youtube.com/watch?v=uZ55mDL7dA0

Help the children sing this simple worship song. If you use the YouTube video, you'll notice it lasts over 10 minutes. To make this a shorter activity or to keep it easy so the children can sing it, fade it out after about 3 minutes. Following that it goes into a beautiful bridge, but it will be harder for kids to sing.

CLOSING MOMENTS   5 Minutes

   Clean Up and Prayer Time

Encourage the children to pick up the markers. Remind them they may have to wait until next week to take their blessing blooms home if they are still wet. Ask them to push in their chairs and gather in a circle. Then close with the prayer below or pray spontaneously.

Dear Jesus,

We praise you that you give blessings. We want to bless others, and we want you to bless others. I ask you to bless these children especially, Lord. The Lord bless you and keep you and make His face to shine upon you and be gracious to you. The Lord turn His face toward you and give you peace.

In Jesus' precious Name, Amen

More Titles in the Sycamore Tree Children's Series

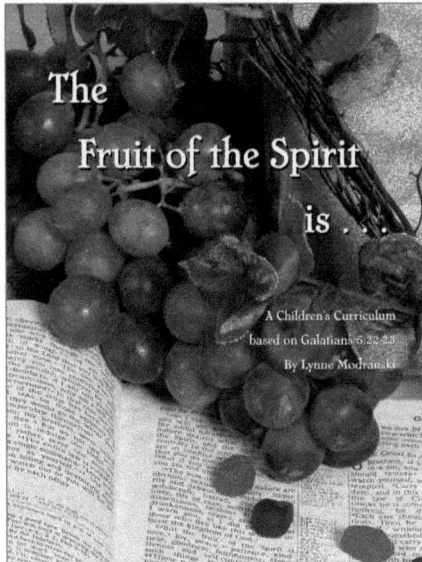

The Fruit of the Spirit is . . .

These nine lessons help children understand the principles of Love, Joy, Peace, Patience, Kindness, Gentleness, Faithfulness, Goodness, and Self-Control. Each uses a different story from scripture to demonstrate the fruit. In addition to easy prepare, Biblically sound lessons, you'll find an original song and plans to create a Fruit Tree to reinforce the theme.

Heroes, Heroines, Champs, and Chumps

Curriculum for a full year. With 13 lessons focused on the Patriarchs, 13 from the Kings and the prophets and 13 from the New Testament, you'll find great examples to help kids grow in Christ. The final fourteen lessons will take you through all the holidays including the seasons of Lent and Advent.

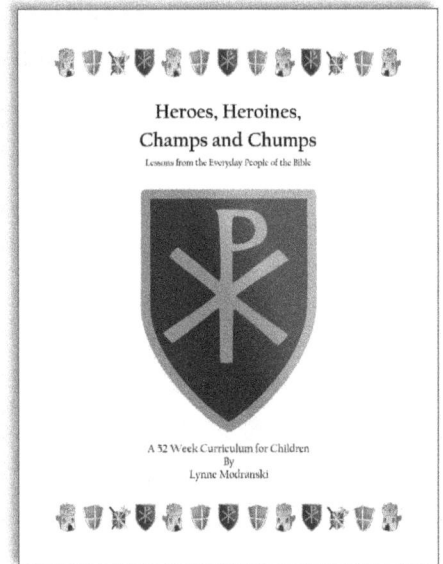

Children of the King

We need more kids with noble traits, kingly traits. These lessons from the life of King David present thirteen opportunities for children to learn how to produce perseverance, faith, courage, self-control, God-reliance, integrity, hospitality, gratitude, humility, repentance and forgiveness.

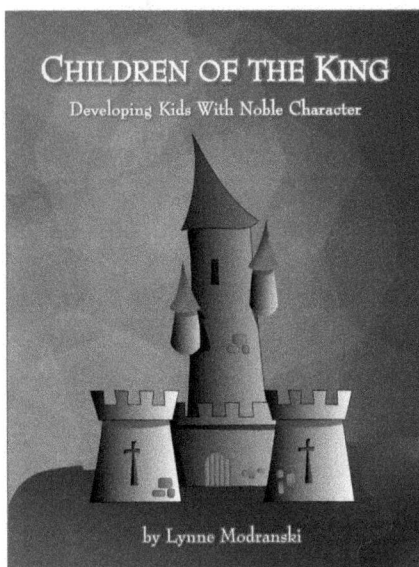

Jesus, Teach Me How to Pray

Help the children in your kids' ministry learn "The Lord's Prayer". Each line offers three lessons to reinforce the message. To round out the year, you'll find lessons to teach the Ten Commandments and the 23rd Psalm. With present day applications that's relatable to kids, these 52 lessons may even help teachers gain a new perspective on these Bible basics.

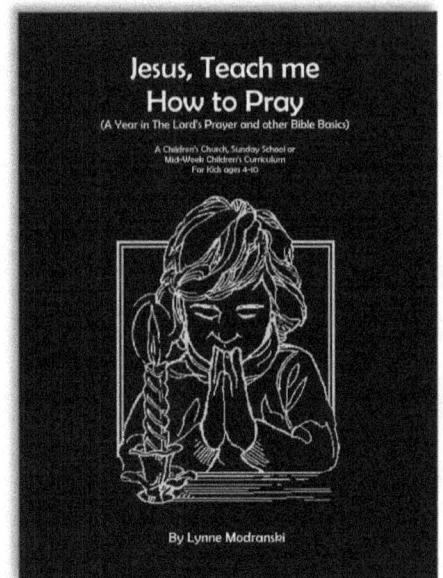

Find them all on my website
www.LynneModranski.com

First Steps for New Christians

Available at www.LynneModranski.com

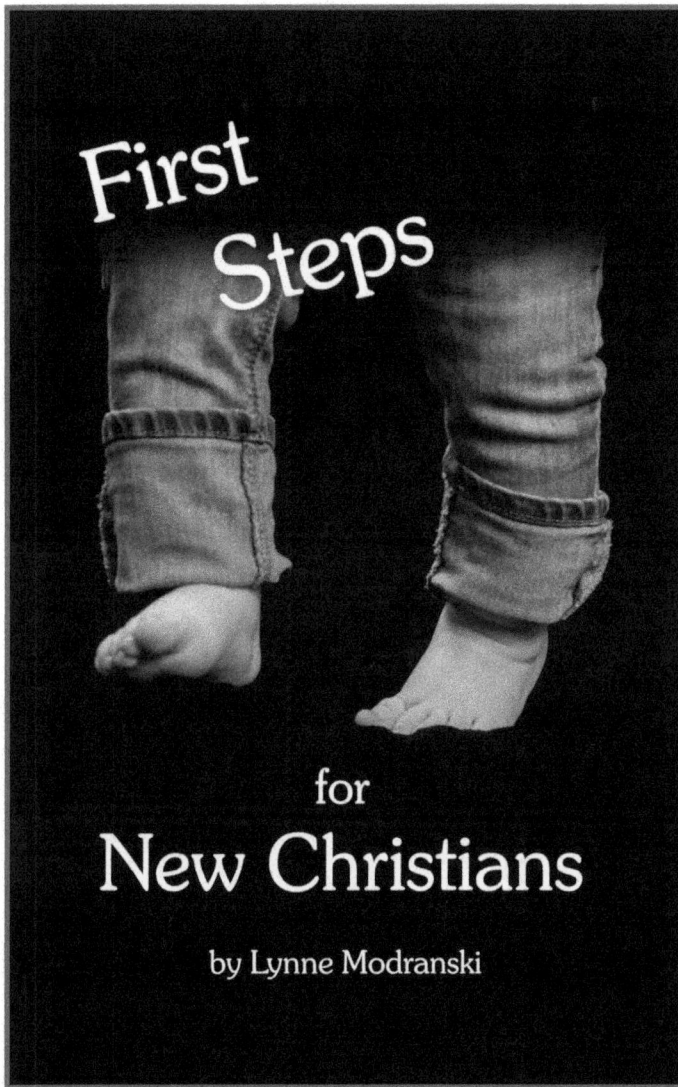

These forty short devotions bring strength to those in the first days of their Christian journey. Even folks who've walked in the faith for years, but feel like their still babes, can benefit.

Each week offers one of the following themes:

- Discovering your True Identity in Christ
- How Much You are Loved
- Finding Hope in the Journey
- Moving from Rules to Relationship
- Building the Relationship
- Accepting the Gifts God wants to Give You

I'm so committed to helping New Christians get a jump start in their walk with Christ that you'll find this e-book free on my website.

Join the First Steps Tribe

In addition to the book, you'll find details on how to join the First Steps Tribe. With a private Facebook group, daily or weekly e-mails and assignments to help young Christians go deeper, the tribe provides accountability and encouragement.

Devotion Books

"Devotions Inspired by Life" and "Devotions for Church Leaders and Small Groups" are just two of the devotion books available in my online store. These two each offer more than seventy devotions meant to inspire and encourage. Each short meditation offers a lesson from life or Biblical insight to empower leaders and inspire those growing in Christ.

Find them on my website:
www.LynneModranski.com

www.ingramcontent.com/pod-product-compliance
Lightning Source LLC
Chambersburg PA
CBHW062052090426
42740CB00016B/3108